From Clouds to Concrete

Starting and Leading a Christian Nonprofit

Cinny Roy

Dedication

Where to begin? Fact and emotion blended together in gratefulness. Every woman who has come to the Eve Center, each volunteer, each investor, all who spoke into my heart, all who challenged me, - thank you. I cannot count all the blessings passed down to me by my paternal grandparents who heard God call them to be missionaries to the Arapaho Indian tribe in the state of Wyoming in the late 1920s. This changed the course of our family. My parents and sisters, my beloved husband Bruce Roy and his siblings and their spouses have given me more than I deserve. Our amazing children have taught me life lessons, for which I am eternally grateful. To each and all of you, this book is dedicated.

I am grateful for:

Nancy, Sharon, and Mona who heard me telling the vision for the Eve Center before the ministry began.

Unsweetened iced tea—the best drink ever (with lemon please!).

Health to exercise and sweat out the pressures of ministry (thank you, Trisha).

The Barrel Babes: Andrea, Barb, Patti, and Vickie who were there since 2000 and have loved me and watched this *thing* called the Eve Center be birthed and grow.

Empathy.

Reova and Sharyl at Center for Women's Ministries for the original model for the Eve Center.

The God-given ability to care deeply for others and the desire to create a new model fitting our culture and community.

Val, Carol, and Wanda who let me talk their ears off and didn't tell me I am too wild or crazy.

Jim M. who has stood alongside as wise counsel for years and has been available whenever I needed a 'sorting out.'

The countless clients who shared their hurts, their desperation, their care.

Gillian and my pre-readers: Bruce, Mary Pat, Monica K, Wanda, Ruth and Scott.

The wounds that Jesus has healed in women at the Eve Center. For His doing it all, all to Him whom I owe the most. And yet, He needs nothing from me but means it all to be for me.

For His grace to me—for all the times I blew it.

Enjoy this thing called life. Revel in the journey and take time to appreciate, delight, love, and relish each season. Then as Lee Ann Womack's song says; "I hope you dance."

Copyright © 2016 by Cinny Roy. All rights reserved.

This book or any portion thereof may not be reproduced or used in any manner whatsoever without the express written permission of the publisher except for the use of brief quotations in a scholarly work or book review. For permissions or further information contact Braughler Books LLC at info@braughlerbooks.com.

Printed in the United States of America

First Printing, 2016

ISBN 978-1-945091-14-8

Ordering Information: Special discounts are available on quantity purchases by bookstores, corporations, associations, and others. For details, contact the publisher at sales@braughlerbooks.com or at 937-58-BOOKS.

For questions or comments about this book, please write to: info@braughlerbooks.com.

Braughler Books
braughlerbooks.com

Contents

Introduction and Purpose......11

History......13

If You Are Considering Starting a Christian Nonprofit, or, If You Are Stalled In Your Ministry......17

How To Use This Book........21

Leadership Life Lessons

1. Affirmation...............23
2. Aging Does Happen......24
3. Alcohol..................26
4. Always Takes Longer......26
5. Anticipation, Not Anxiety #1...........28
6. Anticipation, Not Anxiety #2...........29
7. Armed Forces Model......30
8. Awards And Honors......32
9. Being Obedient Despite The Outcome.....33
10. Boundaries: Do What You Are Trained To Do....34
11. Branding.................35
12. Burnout #1..............36
13. Burnout #2..............37
14. Burnout #3..............39
15. Can I Pray For You?.......40
16. Can't Do It By Myself.....42
17. Check What You Say: "Come Play With Me".....43
18. Check Your Heart For Secret Agendas..........44
19. Committees.............45
20. Complain Or Confess.....46
21. Complaint Department...47
22. Confidentiality, Others...49
23. Confidentiality, Yours.....50
24. Crisis, Or Is It? God Is Moving...........51
25. Crisis: There Are Always Options..........52
26. Crisis: Your Crisis Is Not Another's Emergency.....53
27. Democracy Versus Dictatorship.............55
28. Diagnosis: What We Don't Do...............56
29. Diplomacy..............57

30. Do You Know 'I AM'?.....59
31. Documentation #1........60
32. Documentation #2........61
33. Do Not Cast Pearls Before Swine.............62
34. Donor Levels: Level The Field When You Can......63
35. Don't Assume Anything...64
36. Don't Be An Agist........65
37. Don't Be Sexist...........66
38. Don't Blame Me If You Don't Tell Me.......68
39. Don't Compare...........70
40. Don't Compromise For A Buck.............71
41. Don't Cook The Books....72
42. Don't Drown Others In Your Enthusiasm.......74
43. Don't Expect Too Much...75
44. Don't Hide From What You Don't Know..........76
45. Don't Live In The Margins.77
46. Don't Make The Job Fit The Person. What Is Best For The Organization?.....79
47. Don't Undercut Someone At Their Own Event......80
48. Dress For Respect Not For Effect............81
49. Empty The Trash.........82
50. Engaging The Quiet Ones..84
51. Every Day Matters— The Dash................85
52. Everyone Wants A Piece Of The Action............86
53. Expense Generous, Income Conservative.....87
54. Financial Road Rash......88
55. Flooding.................90
56. Four Main Food Groups...91
57. Gate Crashers: Boundaries..92
58. Get Good Counsel........93
59. Give It Back To God......95
60. Glass Half Empty, Glass Half Full...........96
61. Go Eat Lunch............97
62. God First Always.........98
63. God First? Family First? Which Is It?..............99
64. God Makes It Quite Clear.100
65. God Provides...........102
66. Grace or Consequences..103

67. Great Idea,
    Put It In Writing.........105
68. Grieve................106
69. Guard Hearts, Not Idols..107
70. HALT, My Version.......109
71. Head Knowledge Versus
    Life Knowledge.........110
72. Honor 'No' From The
    Holy Spirit.............112
73. Iced Tea Is Not Working..113
74. If Only: Lottery Thinking.115
75. Incident Management
    And Reporting..........116
76. Insurance: General
    Liability And D&O......118
77. Integrity...............119
78. Is This As Far As
    It Will Go?............120
79. If You Died Tomorrow,
    They'd Have To Figure
    It Out.................121
80. It's Not A Bad Idea,
    It's The Timing.........123
81. Job Description,
    Include Prayer..........124
82. Judge Judy, or,
    Special Cases...........125
83. Keep It Simple.........126
84. Keep Your Eyes Upon
    Jesus—Murray Hastings..127
86. Know Your Kryptonite...128
86. Laugh..................129
87. Leaders Are Human.....130
88. Legacy: Close The Doors
    When It's Time.........131
89. Lesser Strengths........132
90. Letting Go Of Volunteers.133
91. Life And Death Language.134
92. Location, Location,
    Location...............135
93. Loneliness.............138
94. Manipulator:
    Are You One?..........140
95. Message Versus Delivery.142
96. Money Control,
    Whose Is It?...........143
97. Money Does
    Grow On Trees.........144
98. No Drinking On The Job.146
99. Not Always Right.......146
100. Not Even The Christian
     World's Way...........148
101. One Decision Maker;
     A Partnership Doesn't
     Work..................149

102. Organizational Boundaries 150
103. Passion Versus Love 151
104. Passion Versus Skill Set . . . 152
105. Patterns 154
106. People First Always 155
107. Photos And Testimonies . . 156
108. Preparing For Emotional Conversations 157
109. Public Speaking 160
110. Put It In Writing: Agenda And Minutes 161
111. Remembrance 163
112. Say What You Need 164
113. Scout Versus Wagon Train 165
114. Self-image Versus God's Image Of Me 167
115. Sleepless Nights 168
116. Spiritual Road Crash 169
117. Success More Than Anything; Wrong God . . . 170
118. Success Versus Obedience 171
119. Takers 173
120. Thesaurus And Editing . . . 174
121. This Job Is Not All There Is: Heaven 175
122. Threats: External, Outside the Organization 176
123. Threats: Inside the Ministry 177
124. Threats: Internal And Dangerous 178
125. Volunteers: It Costs Them Time And Money To Serve 180
126. Watch Woman On The Tower 181
127. Watch The Um, And Like . 182
128. What's my point? Personal or organizational? Or God? . . 184
129. What's The Point? Lessons To Be Learned . . . 185
130. When It Is Time To Go . . . 186
131. Who Do You Think You Are? 187
132. Who Is Responsible? 189
133. ZZZZ 190
About the Author 191
Index 192

Introduction And Purpose

This book is a collection of day-to-day lessons learned from starting and leading a Christian nonprofit. This is for many men and women who are called by God into ministry. It is my heartfelt desire that readers gain a new nugget of knowledge whether they are considering starting, are in the early stages of building, or are seasoned leaders. There are many excellent leadership-training programs. Successful industry leaders have published volumes of management considerations. I do not have a business degree, a marketing degree, a finance degree, nor a nonprofit leadership certification. The business language was foreign to me as I tried to take time to read and learn early on. When you are so busy caring for, being there for, learning by trial and error, seeking funding, and developing social media—there isn't time to digest much of the years and years of written wisdom on paper or tablet.

According to the National Center for Charitable Statistics (NCCS), more than 1.5 million nonprofit organizations are registered in the US* This number includes public charities, private foundations, and other types of nonprofit organizations, including chambers of commerce, fraternal organizations, and civic leagues.

Your christian nonprofit is one of many. But before God, yours is singular, special, and loved by our Almighty Creator.

Here are easy to read, compare your world to mine, chapters. I value your thoughts and suggestions. You may reach me by postal mail: Cinny Roy, PO 36362, Cincinnati, Ohio 45236 or email: cloudstoconcrete@gmail.com

*http://grantspace.org/tools/knowledge-base/Funding-Research/Statistics/number-of-nonprofits-in-the-u.s

History

Post August 2002

In the summer of 2002, I had one more year of school to complete for my Master's degree in Counseling. Wrestling with what the next move would be following licensure, I sought advice from those who know me well. Everyone said I should continue working in women's issues.

While cutting the grass in August, I talked to God. "There's got to be a way to honor women's walks with You. How to capture their life knowledge and share that with other women? Yet not everyone can or wants to train to be a clinical therapist. How might their wisdom be merged with basic psychology in a Christian setting?" Within two weeks, I received a newsletter in the mail from the American Association of Christian Counselors (aacc.net). It contained a short article about the International Center for Women's Ministries (ICWM) (centerforwomensministries.org) in Bloomington, Indiana. *THAT'S IT!!* was my response. I quickly contacted them and began a conversation about bringing their program to Ohio. In March of 2003, I attended their first leadership-training module. I returned to Cincinnati, finished my thesis, graduated, and took the licensing exam for Ohio. While taking the summer off (yes, even I know when to stop, drop, and rest), the concept of a chapter of ICWM continued. I shared the vision all over (Mona, Nancy, Sharon, anyone who would listen).

I declared September 1, 2003 the founding day of the Eve Center. I had a stack of notebooks, a cell phone, and an old computer; but no Board, no office, no volunteers, no clients—yet.

My father, as pastor at our church, and the elder board understood the vision and gave me two unused rooms on the second floor of our church building. An advisory board of six women joined with me to start planning the first peer counselor training to begin in January 2004. We secured a post office box, a telephone line with internet, and some furniture.

Eve Center opened it doors officially June of 2004 with eleven clients and the first group of volunteer peer counselors. Today, Eve Center has three locations seeing over 120 women a month with strategic plans for further expansion. Each woman is regularly involved in face-to-face peer counseling, attending a book study, or participating in a recovery group. Over 400 volunteers have been trained and have served off and on over the years. There are approximately 50 requests for help each month. Every day we see miracles: women's lives are changing, healing, restoring, and being made new. It is a vertical learning curve with God, and I wouldn't have it any other way.

Pre-August 2002

How did I get to that fateful summer of cutting grass and talking to God about what comes next? The story lies in the depth of love Jesus has for me and how He carefully has ordered my steps since before I was born.

Growing up in Cincinnati, Ohio, I had all the comforts one could want. I was loved by my parents, received a good education, and participated in sports and church. I had friends yet, like many teens, I itched to run my life by my rules.

By the time I reached college I thought I could be my own boss. I was into partying even though I did pray. I made a commitment to Jesus for Him to be my Savior at the age of twelve, but now I considered God a tool in my tool box to use to rescue me when I got into trouble.

Then came a time when I reached a crisis of my own making. At twenty I was pregnant and in shock. I parked my moral code at the curb and secretly got an abortion. I thought that would take care of everything and I could put it all in a mental box on a shelf buried in my subconscious where it would never again be an issue. I could not have been more wrong.

I met and married my awesome husband and we have three amazing adult children. I got involved in their schools, our church activities, and volunteered for many causes. I was immersed in a whirlwind of activity.

In 1996, I was crashing. I could not continue doing it all, trying to be a super Christian woman. I was drowning. I cried out to God "What do You want from me?!" In His gentle, loving way He replied "It is not what I want from you, but for you. It is time to deal with the box on the shelf." That scared me yet I so wanted peace. Little did I realize that I had been trying on my own to be perfect in order to appease God for what I had done.

My denial and my repressed feelings, were all leaking through. I sought confidential help and was directed to HEART, a small Christian nonprofit in the area. Through the recovery group I not only found, believed and received total forgiveness and freedom for my rebellion and behavior, but I now had a new level of trust in God that I had not had before.

God is Holy and full of Grace. The truth is I am not perfect. Nothing in my own strength can equate me with God. Because of my imperfections, I am separated from God who has no imperfections. I could not earn His approval on my own. That is a horrible place to be. Knowing this, God the Son, Jesus, came here for ME and paid my debt since I could not. Jesus took the judgment meant for me because of my horrible behavior, both thinking and acting. Now God sees me perfect and worthy. He created me, laid out a plan for me, waited and watched as I went a different way, met me when I cried out in pain, rescued me, cleaned me up and placed me near Him. To Him I owe it all.

With this new start, I became known in the area as an abortion recovery specialist. I still am. Yet I also realized we are complicated creations of God.

We wound and are wounded in a multitude of ways.

I entered graduate school to receive a Master's degree in Counseling, in order to support men and women struggling with a diverse range of concerns. It was after two years with one more to go that I found myself cutting grass and dialoging with God about what was to be next. So began the vision for the Eve Center.

PONDER: Have you ever felt unworthy because of what you have done or what was done to you?

Have you ever considered getting to know God, Creator, Provider, Healer, the Mighty, Amazing, Loving, Wild, Unchanging God?

What has stopped you?

As you will see in the next section, it may be time for you to challenge God. Ask Him to show you He is who He says He is. Here is a way to do that:

"Jesus, I don't know you well, but I know I haven't done too well on my own. I need more than I am capable of saying, yet You know my heart. Please join me, forgive me, save me. Show me what to do."

Now go tell someone you talked to God. You will never be the same. Oh – and please let me know will you? Email: cloudstoconcrete@gmail.com.

If You Are Considering Starting a Christian Nonprofit, or, If You Are Stalled In Your Ministry

Are you bored? Do you wonder if being a Christian is blah? Do you think God is bland, vanilla, just a list of *don'ts*? Are you a legacy believer—brought into church by a family member and so it's comfortable? Are you a nominal Christian? Sunday is okay; however, you long for more, but once you go to lunch after service, the mood goes away? You want what you see in or hear about others but it would mean changing and things are good enough as is…

Maybe you sense God calling you to be engaged in ministry. You may have a dream He placed in your heart. Maybe you desire to see change because of a struggle you or those you care about have experienced.

Whether you simply want more from life or you have a focus; here are truths to grasp:

THERE IS NOTHING BORING ABOUT GOD. He takes risks; grabs us, and fights for us. He is the ultimate provider of resources. God created everything from nothing by His word. He sees all. He knows all. He is in your world even when you don't know it! How wild is that?

Lesson 1: DARE GOD. This is not a direct challenge; it is a longing, a deep soul desire to mean something, be something, to do something profound. He will answer. When I accepted Jesus as my Savior, something inside me knew that maybe, just maybe, this was a good thing.

God is not crazy—far from it. He is the ultimate thinker. He creates intricate, detailed experiences for you and me.

I am also here to tell you about a crazy, wild, wonderful, vast God who has an intense love for you and me. AND He wants us to be a part of the zany, enthusiastic, growing, loving, expressive, infinite, life both now and forever.

Open your heart and mind and hear this—take it in and then make it yours. Dare God to be BIG to you.

1 CHRONICLES 28:9 'And you…acknowledge the God of your father, and serve him with wholehearted devotion and with a willing mind, for the LORD searches every heart and understands every motive behind the thoughts. If you seek him, he will be found by you.'

Lesson 2: COMMIT. Let your yes be *yes* and your no be *no*. Just say no to distractions of the world. Just say 'no' to anything that is not the focus of the vision God gave you. You must say 'no' to much of the world if you want to be all in with God. Learn to say no—and that applies at every age. 'No' is an ongoing active word. I work at it. '*No*' once isn't good enough.

I have to live the *no to the world* while I am *all in yes to God.*

I was all in—in praise and worship at my church, but at the same time, I wanted to fit in, to have it all. So in high school and college I thought I could party and pray—be the director of my own fate. I had God in my corner so why not have the world too? This got me into a lot of trouble (See Pre 2002). I had to say YES to the ask from God. Dare is a challenge, the courage to do something. Be bold enough to ask God to be bold in your life.

Matthew 6:33 'Seek first his kingdom and his righteousness, and all these things will be given to you as well.'

Psalms 119:2, 10-16 'Blessed are they who keep his statutes and seek him with all their heart; I seek you with all my heart; do not let me stray from your commands. I have hidden your word in my heart that I might not sin against you. Praise be to you, O LORD; teach me you decrees; With my lips I recount all the laws that come from your mouth. I rejoice in following your statutes as one rejoices in great riches. I mediate on your precepts and consider your ways. I delight in your decrees; I will not neglect your word.'

Psalms 37:5 'Commit your way to the LORD; trust in him and he will do this: He will make your righteousness shine like the dawn, the justice for your cause like a noonday sun.'

First: Dare God to show Himself. Second: be all in committed for life, and your life will become ministry.

Lesson 3: BE READY. You do not know when nor what, but you must know that anything and everything has purpose. That purpose is to point to God and give Him worship, honor, praise.

Matthew 25:1-13 'At that time the kingdom of heaven will be like ten virgins who took their lamps and went out to meet the bridegroom. Five of them were foolish and five were wise...' (read the complete passage—which are you?)

Luke 12:35 'Be dressed ready for service and keep your lamps burning, like men waiting for their master to return from a wedding banquet, so that when he comes and knocks they can immediately open the door for him.'

1 Corinthians 2:9 'No eye has seen, no ear has heard, no mind has conceived what God has prepared for those who love him.'

Dare God, Commit and Be Ready for His move in your life.

Lesson 4: ALWAYS ASK GOD. I knew that the vision of the Eve Center was all God's and that He would make it happen. It has been vital, absolute, and foundational that everyone involved in the programs and program support is in conversation with God DAILY, FREQUENTLY. Every aspect of the ministry has been soaked with prayer and praise.

Psalm 86:6-7 'Hear my prayer, O LORD; listen to my cry for mercy. In the day of my trouble I will call to you, for you will answer me.'

Philippians 4:6 'Do not be anxious about anything but in everything by prayer and petition, with thanksgiving, present your requests to God.'

1 Thessalonians 5: 17 'Pray continually.'

Review: **Dare God, Be Committed, Be Ready, and, Pray Continually.**

Lesson 5: DON'T GO IT ALONE. For years at the Cincinnati Zoo there was a video in the Cat House showing how a lioness hunted zebra. The weaker zebra would fall prey to the attack and be killed. Here is an important lesson for leaders. If a leader thinks they are better than the herd they are leading, they will separate themselves. Being an aloof and detached leader draws a laser focus of the enemy that is out to kill and destroy. The downfall of this leader is imminent. If a leader feels they are not good at their role, or, are in pain but keeps it to themselves, they may wander silently away from the protection of the herd. They are distracted and will not see the lurking enemy that will slay them.

God is all about each of us, refining and adding to a talent He put in you and me, while cutting out sinful thinking and behaving. As leaders we think we have to know all. But don't buy that lie. Stay in community in ministry. Be in the herd. Otherwise you become isolated and open for destruction.

Ephesians 5:30 says 'For we are members of his body' (the church community).

Lesson 6: ADMIT, SURRENDER, RECEIVE. There have been times when I didn't get back with God regularly. I wanted to celebrate the high points but not work out the details. The confounding, mysterious part of this is God didn't quit. He works with me and in spite of me. What a glorious, stupendous, gracious strong God we have! I had been going it alone. It is so easy to wander off, casually saying over my shoulder "Okay God, I've got this," only to fall on my face. I had been trying to walk on my knees, getting ahead of God while giving lip service to prayer. Once I admitted my failing, surrendered all to Jesus, I was renewed, restored.

Ephesians 3:16 'I pray out of his glorious riches he may strengthen you with power through his Spirit in your inner being, so that Christ may dwell in your hearts by faith.'

1 Thessalonians 5:16-18 'Be joyful always; pray continually; give thanks in all circumstances for this is God's will for you in Christ Jesus.'

Dare God; Commit; Be Ready; Always Ask Him; Don't Go It Alone; Admit, Surrender, Receive.

And the last lesson: BE CONTENT IN THE STORY.—let God write the chapters

There is a wonderful Hymn, "Here I am Lord" (1981) by Daniel Schutte (b. 1947). It begins with God the Creator seeking whom will respond to His call to join Him in caring for all people. The chorus has the singer answering 'Yes.' I made this hymn the song for my life. I did hear His call on my life. I have gone as He has led me.

God will write the chapters of your story, your ministry.

Don't force it. Watch instead!

Ephesians 3:17a-21 'I pray that you, being rooted and established in love may have power, together with all the saints, to grasp how wide and long and high and deep is the love of Christ, and to know this love that surpasses knowledge—that you may be filled to the measure of all the fullness of God.'

How To Use This Book

This book is comprised of leadership life lessons. They are alphabetical by title. The Index has topical designations for Leadership, Personal, Procedures & Protocol, as well as Relationships with Board, Community & Clients, God and Staff & Team. At the conclusion of each lesson are several questions for the reader to PONDER. Use the space to make notes that you can then APPLY to your life and your leadership.

Leadership Life Lessons

1. Affirmation

The world is a mean place. No matter where you turn it is negative. With twenty-four-hour-a-day news, streaming video of important and nuisance topics, and access to events as they happen, there is judgment and opinion from every corner. Shaming and bullying are loud, constant and mostly factless regardless of the age of the victim or the predator.

Strive to be a person of affirmation. Declare, announce, support, and encourage those all around you. Affirmation is not lying about someone or something. You aren't saying "Ooo I love your dress", or, "Awesome watch dude." Affirmation is lifting up the person created in God's image. God says all humans are created in His image (Genesis 1:27).

There are various ways to accomplish this: public acknowledgement of staff or volunteer accomplishments, welcoming them by saying you are glad to see them or to hear their voice on your phone. Send a card in the mail or an electronic card by computer. Be inclusive. Invite others to be a part of what you are doing. Tell someone who knows the specific person how much you enjoy them. Say "THANK YOU".

We have many volunteers at the ministry. There are those who bring in toilet paper, candy, or paper towels as a donation. We SO appreciate that. Some come just to stuff the newsletter or to pray. Others provide direct care to the clients as peer counselors, book study leaders, recovery group facilitators, and more. The Board is comprised of volunteers. I value every minute they give to guiding the organization. Gifts given from investors in every denomination keep the phone ringing and the doors open. APPRECIATE THEM! It is as simple as looking up and smiling at each person who comes to the offices.

Pour out love and affirmation to those around you. It fills your own soul.

As their leader, they look to you for approval of their work.

PONDER: How can I show my gratitude to:

Volunteers

Donors

Community (churches, other ministries and organizations)

Staff

Family

Friends

God

Other ideas:

Now APPLY.

2. *Aging Does Happen*

When the Eve Center started, I was forty-six-years old. Thirteen years later, I am aware that I do not have the same energy level as when I started. As a woman, I have gone through much of the menopausal cycle while steering the ministry. Several years ago, I noticed my moods were darker. I am a very upbeat person. But the joy was just not there. I paused to think: Was I burned out? Was I tired? Was I doing too much? The events and losses that were happening around me; I *felt* more; I cried more easily. This was not my normal. But like most women and men—I powered through it and kept on going.

Then one day I was in the McDonald's drive through. The line was backed up. I paid for my ice tea without event and pulled up to the delivery window. There was a young man, obviously a new hire, with fear in his eyes. As he handed me my drink I said, "Hang in there, it will be all right." I pulled way, and burst into tears. At that moment, I realized I was not at all my usual self. It is not normal to cry over a fictional issue such as thinking the McDonald's worker was struggling.

At my annual gynecological appointment, my wonderful nurse practitioner asked me if there were any changes. I told her about my emotional down turn. Before I completed the explanation, she had written a prescription. "Here," she said. "You are experiencing what many women do at this point in life. Your biology has swung and you need an anti-depressant/anti-anxiety boost now." Geeez… I am getting old! I am glad I told the truth because I am now back in balance, back to my enthusiastic self.

Pay attention to your body signals. Be self-aware and attend to your physical health. As a leader, model healthiness by having regular physical examinations for general health, "lady parts", dental, eye screening, skin care, as well as whatever else may come through your family tree. MEN: you are aging as well. Attend to visual and audial loss, prostate issues, weight gain: male-o-pause!

PONDER: When was my last medical check-up?

What do I need to do to improve my health so I am a good role model for my ministry?

Other thoughts:

Now APPLY.

3. Alcohol

As a Christian organization, it was important to establish our guideline regarding alcohol. Many women and families have been severely wounded by alcohol abuse. The other end of the spectrum was the viewpoint that it was in the Bible and is to be enjoyed: "Jesus made water into wine "(John 2:1-10) and so it goes. Is it banned from our events? Is it only banned on the premises if we have an open house or small event? Do we serve or allow others to bring it in?

To respect both positions and all in between, the Board wrote this policy:

> *Individuals who would enjoy an alcoholic beverage may purchase such through the event location staff at Eve Center fundraising events. Eve Center staff and volunteers will not be serving alcohol. Closed containers of alcohol (wine) may be included in raffle baskets. A nonalcoholic version will be made available to the winner of said raffle basket (or other prize packaging) if requested. Eve Center's purpose is to encourage all to feel secure and enjoy their experiences at the Eve Center, client programs and fund raisers.*

PONDER: What is the policy of your organization?

Does it need strengthening?

Other thoughts:

Now APPLY.

4. Always Takes Longer

In my mind tasks and projects can all be done in less time than it actually takes. There is no good way to 'hurry up' the planning if it is necessary for best outcomes. I can't help being ready to move on to the next 'thing.' Being a big picture person, I see ahead. Yet it has been vital to the life of the organization that I breathe and allow others to breathe. Inhaling brings oxygen to the brains of those crafting the steps to accomplish much. In my mind I may want to just 'get it done' but at what cost to the ministry, others, and myself? Will my restlessness bring glory to God or deter others from wanting to serve God in the business?

The ministry needed new computers as well as the software to reduce the paperwork for each client. My thinking was to go price computers and get them. Task complete. I was stopped at the door by wise staff. To properly invest for improved functioning, key staff as well as a Board member with expertise in this area needed time to gather data. They were tasked with identifying what specifically needed improvement, who this would impact and proficiencies to incorporate in the selection of new software. Twelve months of process compilation resulted in excellent selection of computers and software. My immediate response was absolutely wrong for the massive undertaking that I underestimated.

Each component of ministry must receive sufficient time to prepare for execution.

PONDER: How do I rush my team?

Is the ministry trying to do too many things? What are they?

Are we attending to the mission or to just doing something new?

Other ideas:

Now APPLY.

5. *Anticipation, Not Anxiety #1*

Having a nervous tummy does not make one a healthy leader. Anxiety comes from not knowing what is ahead, trying to plan for the unknowns and never resting. Anxiety is reduced when planning takes place. A best practice is to have the Board and key leadership participate in SWOT: Strengths, Weaknesses, Opportunities, Threats. In reviewing and identifying issues in each category, fear is reduced, resources are allocated, and preparations made. In addition, sharing candidly with one another builds teams that can celebrate strengths as well as face the challenges ahead. There is information on the internet about SWOT and other helpful planning tools.

As a leader, I, by being transparent about concerns, have found others have similar thoughts. My stepping forward drew the ministry forward. Trust grew within the team and in the structured anticipation.

Turn anxiety into positive expectation.

PONDER: Has the staff or Board spent time reviewing internal and external strengths and weaknesses?

What can I identify right now that are:

Strength

Weakness

Opportunity

Threat

Other ideas:

Now APPLY.

6. Anticipation, Not Anxiety #2

Good planning can offset unexpected situations. At the same time, no one can ever anticipate everything. I can get snarled up in wondering. The *What ifs* can flood my head. What if no one signs up to take the volunteer peer counselor training? What if people stop giving to the ministry? How are we going to do it all? This is based on fear of what I can't control.

Solution #1: Share with other leaders in ministry. Others who have been in leadership can listen and provide guidance.

Solution #2: Talk through fantasy and nightmare thoughts. Find the realistic expectations. When I hit one of these moments, I call it "let's look over the cliff." View the polar ends of the situation. The perfect, glorious outcome would be that there are so many applications for training that we have to either extend it or have a waiting list. This is fantasy thinking. The other end of the spectrum takes me to the edge. For some time we held the training only in the fall. There was a soft deadline for applications several weeks before the first class. With low numbers at the end of July or beginning of August, I would begin to fret. What if we only get a few—will we merge the evening and morning class into one? Will we start later in the month? Can I expect the trainers who are volunteers to give their time for only a few? My mind would spin. Nightmare! If no one comes for training, and the number of volunteers dwindles, then maybe it will be time to close the doors and say job well done. Nothing lasts forever.

Balanced thinking is realistic thinking.

Anxiety can spin one over the edge. Realistically God has called a sufficient number of trainees for every class every time we offer it. I am not in control—I shall do my very best to anticipate what our community needs. We will market what is offered. Reviewing past experience, listening to our audience and then offering to fill the gap is good anticipation of community needs.

EVERY TIME God has blessed us with many new volunteers to train. His timing is perfect. We have not changed our process or broken structural boundaries. We didn't have to struggle. It was a lack of trust in God and a burden of fear that blocked God's peace in me.

Anticipate what you can. Plan appropriately. Be adults. Relax and enjoy the ride. Take all your cares to God and trust He has the outcome!

PONDER: What part of the ministry causes me to fear?

When have I seen God meet all my needs and more?

What do I need to anticipate and plan for?

How can I pray going forward? What do I need to tell God to invite Him into the process?

Other thoughts:

Now APPLY.

7. Armed Forces Model

As a Christian ministry we do not want to get ahead of what God is saying. Also we do not want to be disobedient to what He directs. Here is the model I have developed to explain excellent obedience.

CALL: The old slogan "Uncle Sam wants you" is just how God calls us. He invites us to be a part of what He is doing in this amazing world. I respond with "Yes, Lord," and move to be near Him. I DO NOT go 'out there' and do what I imagine He wants. I haven't stopped to listen to Him. I MUST stop and LISTEN. God, through prayerful listening, shares the vision He has specifically designed for me.

EQUIP: Again I DO NOT rush to go do what God said because I didn't wait long enough to know HOW He has planned the mission. I STAY STILL. The Lord then equips me with skills, knowledge, and practice so I may be obedient to what He called and showed me to do.

Psalm 46:10: 'Be still and know that I am God."

WAIT: Then I wait at base camp. This calls for patience because my humanness is ready NOW. Like any general, God has more knowledge, more omnipotence, more omniscience than I could ever imagine. He alone knows when I am to move out of camp. There may be others who need clarity of mission and equipping. So I wait for His order to go. I attend to what I have been trained in: communication, relationships, prayer, and intercession, always with an ear to hear.

OBEY: When the order comes, I stick to His plan and not my way of doing things. If I do it my way—well, let's just say I have been around the desert of hard life choices a few times. Have you ever been blown about, feeling directionless, pelted by sand storms of questioning and bombardment by others? It is not pleasant to serve in this manner, but it is the result of my doing it "my way." When I do life and leadership as my loving and orderly Lord designed, then the operation goes well. I am not exhausted, and the execution happened according to God's timing.

REST: Once the assignment is complete, it is key that I return to base camp, to the of throne of God, praising Him for His good leadership. THEN I rest and wait for His next call, equipping, timing, action, and celebration.

PONDER: How have I gotten ahead of God in ministry?

What were the results?

How can I incorporate listen-equip-wait-go-rest into my routine?

Other thoughts:

Now APPLY.

8. Awards And Honors

Our world is full of plaques and trophies. Daily someone is being honored for their accomplishments. Bravo! These are well deserved. It is such a pleasure to be nominated and receive recognition for hard work. If you are nominated fine, but don't make that your goal. Many of the prized accolades are driven by the engine of self-promotion. Most require some paperwork, if not a campaign for endorsements. Then your organization will bear the cost to attend the award ceremony. It is very nice to be recognized by your peers. Often though it is just affirmation machinations, so don't desire it, it is a time drain.

If your organization truly wishes to honor someone, do it without cost to that person or with a cumbersome application process. Honor simply and with words. The person will appreciate it. If as a leader you are feeling unappreciated, seek affirmation but not in a self-centered arena. Go back to the identity that God gave you. You are a beloved son or daughter of our Creator God, the most amazing One, who cares about everything that matters to you. There is nothing and no one who can love you, appreciate you, and have more joy in you than God does.

There are benefits to awards as they are certainly deserved. At times this is a good way to generate publicity about the ministry. Have a balanced perspective going forward.

PONDER: Do I feel appreciated in my work?

Is it important to our credibility that my organization receive awards?

Do I really understand what God says about me?

Other ideas:

Now APPLY.

9. Being Obedient Despite The Outcome

I know God told us what He wanted and we followed through on His leading. Why didn't it turn out as He directed? CORRECTION: He directed me and the ministry leadership to communicate with a specific church for a new location. He did NOT guarantee we would move there. I have had my hand slapped (similar to the two by four to the noggin) by my good God when I have thought I knew what He was thinking. He is clear and not misleading. The misstep comes when I "take it from here" and go ahead without Him. Watch out for distorted thinking any time you have been directed by God regarding the ministry.

We were obedient. The name of the church was given to us by a trusted friend of the ministry. The pastor and leadership team were welcoming. We easily interacted with them. The questions posed by the pastor and team indicated the potential for a mutually beneficial partnership was on the horizon. Then they said no. So who was wrong? We did what God said. EXACTLY. We were obedient. The lesson here is to be obedient despite the outcome. We were not happy. But

it isn't about being happy, it is about trusting that God is and will be in control and has the best in store for us.

So no finger pointing, just back to seeking God's goodness and next steps.

PONDER: When have I questioned God about the outcome of some part of the ministry?

Were we obedient to His lead?

What has been the change since?

Do I and my staff or Board have the same trust level in God as before?

Confess this to Him. Ask for another lesson on trust.

Other thoughts:

Now APPLY.

10. *Boundaries: Do What You Are Trained To Do*

It is vital to stick to what you know and stay away from what you do not know. Every person who joins your work has a skill set. Every person who joins your work has life experiences that are rich and to be shared, but not all of that is beneficial to the role they have.

Your organization may receive a call for help to find housing. Your worker may be asked for insight as to whether to get a divorce, or how to handle a difficult child. We recognize that we are part of the community team. We are not the only game in town and do not have all the answers.

It is critical not to cloud the functions of your ministry.

Well intended assistance can place an organization at risk. Insurance does not cover things done outside the scope of the mission.

We developed a page of what we do not do such as legal, housing, or medical support. Communicate this to your worker bees so they do not feel they have to have knowledge about these things but are equipped with a list of answers: which agencies to refer to where expertise can be found. Have available a list of resources for the most frequently asked questions outside your ministry's area of expertise. Point to the other professionals in your area. They have the knowledge for the questions that are outside your mission. If, and only if, one of your workers is a certified professional do you ask for insight to pass to the inquiring client.

PONDER: Do we blur the lines of job descriptions with personal wisdom in a way that can jeopardize the ministry?

When have I expected the team to assist beyond their skill set?

What training is in place about this?

Other ideas:

Now APPLY.

11. *Branding*

This is not about getting a tattoo. It is about attention spans. It is easier to remember a nonprofit if it has a good logo and clear graphics. Think about what will set your organization apart yet represent your purpose. Invest in a design that is both print-ready and pixel ready for computer work. Do the same for your fund raising events. Repetition is important for folks to remember and respond to your programs and your events. Put the same ministry graphic on EVERYTHING: stationary, website, invitations, thank you notes, Facebook page, T-shirts, all marketing, and publicity. Attach it in jpeg format to anything you wish to be published belonging to another's media. Any materials you prepare should be stamped with the identifying graphic

Include your motto or mission in verbal introductions, testimonies, speeches, trainings, and announcements. Teach it to your Board, your volunteers, key leadership, and staff. The mission statement should be one or two sentences that anyone can memorize. The name of your non-profit should be easily recognized. Often when I am introduced or meet someone and they discover I am part of Eve Center, they say "Oh, I have heard of the Eve Center!" Use this opportunity to share the mission statement and a brief ministry success. Communication is very important. You know what you do, but who else does?

Branding has to do with memorable catch phrases and memorable logos.

Seeing things at a distance or reading what has small print or too many details can be difficult. Keep it simple and visible, yet catchy.

PONDER: What is your elevator speech – the one to two sentences explaining your organization?

Is marketing in the budget? What needs to change to spread the word:

internally to your followers?

externally to the greater citizenship?

Other ideas:

Now APPLY.

12. Burnout #1

One of my sayings is "God and iced tea and I am good to go." But there are days when my mental elevator does not reach the top floor. I just can't focus, or I just don't want to attend to the tasks at hand. I don't even want to go out to lunch, and I LOVE that. These are signals that I need time off. This is different from regular days off. These alerts mean NOW. For my mental health, and so I don't bite anyone, I take a half day or a whole day. I am not going to accomplish much so I have learned to let go. If I can, I rearrange my schedule and just shut down. I putter around the house, read something that has no nutritional value to my brain (women's magazines are brain candy), and just zone alone.

It is important not to guilt myself for this. Starting, leading, and sustaining a ministry is exhausting at times. When I need time off, I NEED time off to recharge. You need time off as well. So follow my example and just enjoy it. Vacate your mental silos for a time. You are not super human. You are not God.

Preventing full burn out is wisdom and not worthy of a single guilty thought.

PONDER & APPLY: When have I needed time off?

Did I take a necessary break to recharge? Why or why not?

Can I give myself permission to take a pause for time to recharge? Why or why not?

Other thoughts:

Now APPLY.

13. Burnout #2

Have you ever been around someone who is burnt out? They look tired and act tired. The response to interaction is delayed or deadened. Or the opposite is witnessed: frantic, snarky, biting replies. There is another version: too happy, too wound up, laughs at everything, full throttle almost manic. Do not become any of these persons! Review the symptom list here and SERIOUSLY assess yourself.

Signs of impending burnout:
- Irritability
- Emotional exhaustion

- Feelings of isolation
- Isolation
- Returning to old coping methods that are not healthy
- Abuse of alcohol or drugs
- Reduced personal effectiveness
- Indecisiveness
- Inability to leave client concerns behind when away from Center
- Compulsive work patterns
- Drastic changes in behavior
- Narrowing of focus
- Not taking time off
- Failure to listen to friends, family and coworkers when they tell you that you seem stressed out, overloaded, tired, etc.
- Not feeling appreciated
- "Refusal to step away"

We become unbalanced when we have:

- Fragile self-esteem
- Difficulty establishing connectedness in personal life
- Increased need to rescue clients
- Assuming it is up to me to heal the person
- Need for reassurance from client
- The work becomes all-consuming like a new love: "emotional affair"

A person who has balance in ministry is:

- Secure in their identity which comes from God
- Invests and maintains friendships and family outside of the ministry
- Respects clients have the right to choose to accept or reject assistance
- Receives affirmation through daily relationship with God
- Has good boundaries, leaves work at work

PONDER: Check all the above symptoms that apply to you.

If five-plus are checked, watch yourself and schedule time away from ministry.

If more than ten are checked, take this very seriously and seek support immediately.

Note the last time you intentionally stopped your brain from working.

What do you like to do to unwind? Plan for that and do it.

To remain an asset to your organization, pamper and protect your biggest asset — YOU!

Other thoughts:

Now APPLY.

14. Burnout #3

It is vital for the health of your organization that you are in tune to your team's stability. Any one of your team may exhibit the afore-mentioned symptoms of burnout. They may be in crisis and overtly or silently suffering.

Be mindful. Slow down and place yourself in the path of your team members. Ask how they are, then listen. Tone, body language, excusing, eye contact, pat answers – wait for the defenses to be lowered.

Ask them the same questions that are in Burnout #1 and #2. Affirm them, care for them, honor them. If you become aware that all is not well with this precious person, make an appointment to talk further and build a plan with them for time to recharge, change assignments, share tasks, problem solve not just problem point.

At the ministry we have a category for when a volunteer needs to take time away. It is called 'AOL: Active on Leave.' This can be a health issue, work, family, anything that needs their full attention. This is granted for three months with a review as to whether they can return to fully participating again. This ensures to them we value them and desire them be free to address priorities of their life.

PONDER: How does my organization address burnout or other conflicts of the team?

Am I as the leader aware of the struggles of my team?

What is needed to change?

Other thoughts:

Now APPLY.

15. *Can I Pray For You?*

Field trips—I loved them when I was in school. We went to the Lollipop Concert series of the Cincinnati Symphony. We would board the yellow school bus and drive WAY downtown. It was a glorious event.

As the leaders of a nonprofit, we visit other organizations, churches, businesses, and individuals. Often we are there to learn what they do, share what we do, and find common ground for growth. One of the things we do every time is offer to pray for and/or with those we visit. It is wonderful to see the peace that descends. A relaxing of expectations happens. Almost always there is a positive response – a moment for thought to articulate the heartfelt need or a quick answer given to us. And we do it right there, right then. We pray. Many are grateful; some have tears. A sigh, an acceptance. We depart shortly, returning to our own sphere of influence.

Be bold. Offering a depth of heart is much more important than the reason you are there.

Our world is dying from a lack of affirmation. Reality prevents us from having regular contact with every person that impact the ministry. Yet we have a powerful way to pour into them: prayer.

1. Pray for your Board, your staff, your volunteers, donors, clients.
2. Pray for the churches who offer support.
3. Pray for the vendors who fill you contracts.
4. Pray for the neighborhoods where your programs are located.
5. Praise God for each of them.
6. Whoever God brings to mind, pray for them.
7. Pray for ministries like yours. Ask God to bless them abundantly. Every organization needs leaders, funders, volunteers and favor in their area of concern.

PONDER: Do I pray for the meetings on my schedule?

Do we pray at meetings and programs?

Do we pray for each other in my organization?

How can my ministry reach out to others in our community in prayer?

Other ideas:

Now APPLY.

16. Can't Do It By Myself

Have you ever heard the saying, "Who died and made you god?!" Well, apply it to yourself. No one will ever do it exactly as you do. No one will ever understand what it is like to have the vision God gave you for the start of this ministry. 'No one' includes YOU.

God is the One who placed this calling in your heart, mind, and soul. He is the One who can do all things because God is God. He does equip you and me to do our very best, through Christ. So humble yourselves, dear brothers and sisters, and ask for assistance. A *Cinnyism* is this:

"Wise men and women take advantage of every resource available. Only fools go it alone."

PONDER: When do I think I am the best at this?

Do I acknowledge and praise God for the vision, the opportunity to serve in His ministry?

Am I delegating or holding all things close out of fear that others will fail my vision?

What needs to change?

Other thoughts:

Now APPLY.

17. Check What You Say: "Come Play With Me"

I have goofy sayings. Sharing about all the wonderful programs of the ministry, I often say "Come play with me." To me this simply means we have joy in what we do and the listener is invited to be a part of it. While the lives of the women we assist are often quite tragic, we are not all down in the face and dragging the cares of the clients on our shoulders around the office. I desire for many to experience God transforming lives by volunteering their time, talent, or treasure. What a saying may mean to me does not always translate the same way to others.

To some the term "Come play with me" has a not so morally appropriate leaning. I never want even a hint of impropriety about what I do or what the ministry stands for to deter others from getting involved. When a caring volunteer brought the double meaning to my attention, I purposefully reviewed my intention. My intention, as mentioned is pure – to have fun in the work of the ministry. Yet if this saying is viewed as a stumbling point for her, it may be for others as well. So I now refrain from using these words in my enthusiastic invitation to engage with us.

Minor issue? Maybe. Yet a good leader listens to all comments and takes to heart what is offered for their consideration.

PONDER: Do I have my ears open to receive insight regarding my words and behavior?

Am I dismissive to these challenges?

What needs to change?

Other thoughts:

Now APPLY.

18. Check Your Heart For Secret Agendas

Four things can destroy a business: money, sex, reputation, and lies. Even if God has ordained the ministry, secret agendas can ruin it. If your success is determined by the size of the budget, cozy relationships with prominent people in the community (church and otherwise), being known by important people, or being bigger and better than, then eventually the truth will be known. Do you want to prove something? Do you want to make up for something? Will you enhance the statistics or inflate the numbers? Any of what is listed makes your agenda your god and the underlying driving force of what you do and how you lead. You are simply using and exploiting the ministry for your own needs. Be careful. Humble yourself and confess to the one who you trust, one who cares about you as well as the organization.

Do not trifle with God.

PONDER: What are my motives for being in this ministry?

Right now ask God, who knows you better than you know yourself, anything and everything that makes you a threat to His work in the ministry.

What did God show you?

What needs to change?

Who do you need to assist you in redirecting your motives, better known as accountability?

Other thoughts:

Now APPLY.

19. *Committees*

Everyone wants to engage and experience blessings by giving back in some way. This can be experienced through committee work. What is a committee? A committee is a group of people appointed for a specific function and time of service for the ministry. As a leader at times it may seem to be more time efficient to just complete the work myself. Yet God designed us to be in community. In ministry, committees are one form of community.

Here are six suggestions for effective committees:

1. Have a well-defined objective that is clearly conveyed to the committee members. Make sure the objective supports the vision and mission.
2. Meet regularly with meetings placed at regular intervals on the calendar especially if action steps are to be taken quickly. Early in the formation of the committee the meeting dates are established so all know the dates they are expected to attend.
3. Require a minimum of three members and not more than seven. If the objective is too broad, then break the committee into task groups.
4. Committee chairpersons are most effective when they volunteer rather than appointed. This bridges an understanding of where the objective of the committee fits into the operations of the ministry.
5. Chairpersons should report the committee's progress at every Board of Directors meeting. This keeps the committees on task, and on time to reach the objectives.
6. A chief executive should serve only in an ex-officio position to the committee, not a voting position.

PONDER: How has my organization utilized committees?

What committees worked well and which did not?

What have been my personal experiences of being on a committee?

What do I need to do as a leader to have more efficient use of the time and talent of the committees in place?

Does my organization or its Board need training on the purpose and structure of committees?

Other:

Now APPLY.

20. Complain Or Confess

Sometimes I just need to let it out. This is different from seeking wise counsel regarding the growth of the organization. This is personal. There are times when as a leader, I feel I have blown it and desire to share it without having to "be a leader." I just want to be the vulnerable, fallible with no repercussions. There are times when I am tired of being a leader. Or I am feeling threatened. Or I don't feel good enough. Or I question how I handled someone. I need to tell someone without having it all verbally packaged up professionally. I need to be messy and emotional. Find one or two people who care about you, and with whom you feel safe. Explain what you desire from the relationship, what you need. Do you need to just talk and have the person listen? Do you need affirmation? Do you need prayer? Is accountability important? The give and take about this will allow for the times you reach out to be mutually beneficial. You will feel listened to, and the receiver of your sharing will know they are doing what is beneficial for you.

Confession is so important. The Bible tells us to bring it to God. Bring it to God by getting it all out with a trusted friend. Then pray together. Do ask your prayer partner to check on you from time to time.

PONDER: Who do I have that I can turn to in whatever shape I am at that moment?

Why did I select this person?

If I do not have a safe person, why not? Who can I reach out to to establish this kind of friendship?

What are the seasons in my work when I need a bit more counsel, support, and to care?

Write out what I need in this new relationship.

Other ideas:

Now APPLY.

21. *Complaint Department*

Who are the customers of your organization? We have two consumer groups. The *first* are our volunteers. We pour into them training, mentoring, oversight, advanced training, prayer, and sisterhood – all so they are healthy models serving as Volunteer Peer Counselors. The more we give to them, the better they care for our other customer group: the clients who come through our doors for care.

It is important to have a feedback process. This is another term for receiving complaints and compliments. If we are to improve our programs, we need to joyfully receive suggestions. Sometimes the language or demeanor of the person providing the feedback makes it feel more like a reprimand or insult. But remember to

look past the delivery to the intent.

First, take the conversation out of public dialogue. DO NOT have the interchange on social media. Move it to private email back and forth. Best practice is to meet with the person face to face. Keep in mind the person may blind copy others to have they 'see' how they are treated by you.

Thank the person for caring about the vision and mission. Share you will give their comment some thought.

There have been times when the customer was very wrong. Still, accept what is said. If they require correction, Take TIME to prayerfully ponder what to say. Then don't say it, write it. This documents what you were told, and how you replied. It shows you took what they said seriously enough to address it professionally and did not reply in a huff of emotion.

If the person is extremely challenging, ask them to put their concerns in writing so you may take it to the other leaders and to the Board. Having to write out the issue provides time for contemplation by the challenger. Having to write out the issue may reduce the venom since it will reflect on the writer. Remember, you do not have to respond to someone who is personally abusive other than to say "Now is not the time to discuss this. Let's meet soon." This diffuses the confrontation.

Over the years I have had volunteers, clients, donors, community, family, and friends say things to me in ways that were not exactly appreciated. If I took it personally, I would have quit long ago. Focus on the mission and how what is being said can improve what is glorifying to God in all you and others do.

PONDER: How do I respond to challenges from various persons encountered in the ministry?

How can I train the staff to have a consistent response to compliments and complaints?

What process needs to be put in place for these situations?

Other ideas:

Now APPLY.

22. *Confidentiality, Others*

Whether at work or at home, what a coworker or friend shares in confidence must be honored and held in confidence. Remember it is up to the other person to determine when, with whom and to what degree their story is shared. I have the honor of hearing many women's stories within the organization and without; women who tell me about professional, personal, and familial struggles and joys. It is not my right to tell anyone else what I have been told. Even if I relate a success, I am careful not to give names because the success often comes from a wound, a loss, or, a one-done-to-another event. Never do you or I want to bring harm to someone or expose a situation that a family member or friend is not privy to. I do not know who knows who. I do know ***every city is a small town*** **when it comes to the underbelly of our souls.**

    I often ask "Do I know this?" meaning is she telling just me, a few friends, or is this now or soon to be public knowledge? There have been plenty of times a mutual acquaintance has told me what I thought was private. I do not break confidentiality even then by saying something like "Oh you know too? Well when she told me…" CONTINUE to be subdued in your response until you know that what is said is intended to be shared. This also deflates the gossiper as they do not get the response they are looking for: that you either know or that they bring you worthy intelligence.

PONDER: How do I protect the confidences others give me?

Am I quick to repeat and enhance a story in the telling?

Do I seek the *'juice'* in order to sound *'in the know'* with others?

Does my team see me as a safe person with which to confide? Why or why not?

Have I ever had my trust broken and something told that I held sacred?

How do I instill this in my team?

Other thoughts:

Now APPLY.

23. *Confidentiality, Yours*

I needed someone to talk to. But it wasn't an issue I could take to the Board or other staff members. I was struggling with trusting someone connected to the ministry. I did not want to affect anyone else's perception of that person who would work or volunteer with them. I also did not want to cause any division or cast suspicion. It was important to me to have someone I felt safe with but who would be honest and objective, yet caring. Prayer and listening was first. I did plenty of that. Yet I realized I need the body of Christ to hear me, pray with me, and offer wisdom for consideration. I contacted a pastor and his wife who knew of but were not involved in the ministry. I shared my struggles and desire to learn for myself, and to see God's hand in next steps.

Slowly, with careful steps, I guided the struggle that could have been huge and destructive resulting into a separation of the person who was poisonous from the ministry. I stayed focused on the mission. I had to keep my own counsel with the aid of these two people. They were vital to my health as a leader during that season.

Choose carefully those with whom you can be open: choose persons who are biblically sound, affirming, supportive, wise, yet not someone who has all the answers. God met us in those meetings. Most of all I left intact—not attacked, with good substance to ponder and apply.

PONDER: Where do I go when I need confidential leadership wisdom?

How have I handled intense struggles in the organization?

Am I insane: have I been responding in the same way about this issue, repeating the same actions over and over expecting a different outcome?

What do I need to put in place in anticipation of the time I am struggling?

Other thoughts:

Now APPLY.

24. *Crisis, Or Is It? God Is Moving*

There was a season when several of the key leadership and staff informed me they were stepping down from involvement in the ministry. Over a six-week period, each notified me the change was immediate. When faced with a swell of change, I determined not to go into crisis mode or to take it personally. Yes, personal and organizational reflection is appropriate. Intentional review took place with the Board. What I am noting here is at the time this happened, it was NOT the time to fall apart. I know that when above-normal number of shifts rise up, more than likely

God is bringing change that He has ordered.

It is a time to cling to the Lord and weather the changes. This radical shift brought about needed improvement to roles for staff as well as an opportunity, for new engagement of women who desired to learn and step into leadership. The four who left these roles are sisters in Christ. Each heard our God call her to a new adventure. Changes, seen and unseen, can be trusted as being good because we have a good God who desires the best, even if it seems to be a crisis. Don't give in to a 'woe is me' attitude.

PONDER: Do I intentionally praise God for both the highs and the lows in ministry?

Is it my nature to fall apart when faced with a crisis at work?

How do I handle a crisis?

How can I view these challenges as a chance to grow myself and the ministry?

What preparation can the staff or lead team put in place having learned from a crisis or in anticipation of a crisis?

Other thoughts:

Now APPLY.

25. Crisis: There Are Always Options

In a crisis we have to find the balance point nearer the middle.

Extreme terms like ALWAYS, NEVER, NO ONE are over-the-cliff talk. It usually indicates fear is present. So back away from the cliff and look at the facts: What plans are in place? Are realistic expectations in place? What are the options?

Crisis look differently to each organization. It can be a death of a staff member or resignation of a majority of the board. It can be a decrease in donations, a law suit, a lack of clients, a slipin confidentiality.

In reviewing these, what is the worst that can happen? This the time to be a steady leader. It is not the time to behave as if the ministry is sinking into failure. Say to yourself and repeat to others:

There are always options, especially with a great God.

This is not denial that a crisis is happening. It is about framing the situation as fixable rather than a failure. Correction involves fact; failure focuses on emotion.

Contain the crisis. Communicate to the Board President. Call in prayer. Coordinate and respond. Counsel the staff. Review and relax.

PONDER: What is the protocol for onsite crisis such as fire?

How do I do this?

Other thoughts:

Now APPLY.

26. Crisis: Your Crisis Is Not Another's Emergency

There have been times when I have not thought through what preparation is needed prior to a meeting or an event. While it usually works out, I can be very stressed and have expectations of others involved that are unjust. Quarterly newsletters are mailed in bulk. With over 1,000 envelopes to be prepped (applying address sticker and address label, labeling return address envelope, stamping, printing and collating several pages), a full week is needed. Volunteers need to be asked to participate. There is a date by which I desire the newsletter to be released. The newsletters contain time-sensitive information about training sessions, book studies, recovery groups, and more. My crisis arises when I wait too long to write the content. Then it has to be laid out with graphics and edited before it can be printed. All this needs to be completed *yesterday*. I get frustrated when volunteers don't show up, the edits don't come back quickly enough for me, and the newsletter goes out late. But see? I create the crisis and then expect everyone to jump over my bar. That is not fair. Lesson? Get it done in a timely fashion. Lead by example. Don't take advantage of others just because they are devoted to you.

PONDER:

Where do I procrastinate in my work?

Whom do I lean on too much to cover my work as well as his?

Whom do I need to apologize to and ask for accountability rather than a bail out next time?

What task needs to be deleted from my list in order for the priorities to have my full and timely attention?

Other ideas:

Now APPLY.

27. Democracy Versus Dictatorship

There is a fine balance between being the only one who makes decisions and pluralistic decision-making.

A successful leader sets the parameters for discussion with an intention for the outcome.

I steer toward a goal not necessarily including the exact steps. For instance, the goal in committees is to always be furthering the mission of the ministry. Therefore, the purpose of any committee should directly correspond to the mission. How the goals are achieved is up to the individuals tasked with leading the committee. A good leader affirms the committee or division leaders as they learn how to lead and accomplish their tasks. I demonstrate approval by my presence at meetings from time to time and by my availability. I do not need to articulate my 'yea' or 'nay' for every step.

Do not expect blind obedience. To model a culture of growth in a non-profit, it begins with me being a part of the team working toward fulfillment of the mission, not a dictatorial one-way flow chart of tasks that makes everyone guess what I want. That exhausts everyone and does not keep them coming back to give of their time and talents.

Yet be ready to be the decision maker. There are times when it is my responsibility to steer toward a better choice for the mission of the ministry. Be sure you have established the desired outcome and know consciously what the outcome is to be. Once a year is the leadership summit at the ministry. Attending is the Leadership Team which consists of Staff and Volunteers in key positions. It is a time to review the strategic plan set by the Board, and define individual goals for each department of the organization. Then the Associate Director meets with each Site Manager monthly to evaluate growth.

It makes it easier on your teams if they know what the goals are. You are tasked with the vision and seeing it materialize. You will stand before your Board, investors, community, and God as to how the resources, and the talents of the ministry are invested for the mission.

Leading identifies the exact direction. Guiding gives options.

Enjoin others on how to achieve the results but dictate the results to be achieved.

PONDER: What is my leadership style?

How am I perceived by my team (ask them for input)?

Am I clear in the expectations I place before staff and committees?

Do I hold my team accountable for outcomes? Do we together evaluate progress and formulate next steps?

Am I more a team member or a dictator? How can I grow the leadership muscle needed for balance?

Other thoughts:

Now APPLY.

28. Diagnosis: What We Don't Do

When defining what your ministry is, it is helpful to determine the limits of services. For example: Is financial assistance provided? Do the clients include minors? If minors are clients, are they children, tweens, or teens? What demographic area is served? Are the services provided for a fee or for free? What does your organization provide that others do not? What licensing requirements are necessary?

Just as a doctor rules out diseases and illnesses to make a diagnosis, you and your advisors shape the model by what is not within the vision. It will be clearer for all and provide cleaner communication to investors and the community when you specify this ministry provides needed programs not previously covered. It will keep the focus on the purpose and reduce chances of getting off track.

PONDER: What don't we do?

What do we do that is different from other ministries in our area?

Ask friends outside the ministry to tell you what it is about?

What communication needs to change?

Other ideas:

Now APPLY.

29. Diplomacy

It is vital that as a leader you carefully select the words you speak. Practice choosing words that express affirmation and not negativity. Lift up others by what you say. This is different than flattery. It is an expression of what is good at any given time. Remember at all times you are being observed and what you say may be repeated. In ministry a leader may struggle with board members, volunteers, donors, community, clients, and staff. Therefore, select your words wisely. Direct a conversation toward a positive outcome. Protect the personhood of whom you are talking with or about.

For example: A person approached me right after I had shared my personal testimony in front of a church audience. I had provided the story behind the vision for the ministry. Anyone who does this, experiences a level of vulnerability at the time. "You do this all the time—I can't believe you got the name of so-and-so wrong. What were you thinking...ha, ha, ha" she said in a very pointed tone. There was no missing the derision in her voice. My internal instinct was to burst into tears. I was hurt and offended. This person had come at me before. This time I was prepared.

I inhaled and carefully replied: "Thank you for bringing that to my attention. I will make a note. Pray with me that this mistake does not cause anyone to miss what God has done in my life."

This response left both of us intact; the relationship was still good, and the mistake acknowledged.

The interaction also gave a positive example for others who were present. A secular response could have put her down, berated her for attacking me, etc. Would God have been raised up by that action? I doubt it. So practice diplomacy. Train volunteers and place it in the on-boarding instructions for new hires.

PONDER: How do I handle attacks of this nature?

What do I need to practice as ways to reply to offensive communicators?

Are there other ways to avoid situations that are uncomfortable?

How can I model this for my team?

Other thoughts:

Now APPLY.

30. Do You Know 'I AM'?

God as a three letter word will not carry you through all the highs and lows, all the clouds and concrete of leadership. It is vital that you have a deep, soul knowing understanding of the vastness of God the Father, God the Son and God the Holy Spirit.

Here are a few of the names of God as found in the Bible:

Advocate: 1 John 2:1	Peace: Judges 6:24
All Seeing: Genesis 16	Provider: Genesis 22:14
Almighty: Revelation 1:8	Refuge: Isaiah 25:4
Everlasting: Psalm 90:1	Righteous: Jeremiah 33:16
Guide: Psalm 48:14	Rock: Deuteronomy 32:4
Light of the World: John 8:12	Shepherd: Psalm 23:1
LORD God: Genesis 2:4	Teacher: Matthew 26:18
Mediator: 1 Timothy 2:5	Truth John 14:6

Press into God. As you increase your time with Him, out of your mind and heart will flow His truth, His wisdom, His discernment for leading the ministry. We must be amazed by God in order for praise to come from us to Him. The battle cry of every leader must be 'Praise the LORD!' This is the weapon for casting out doubt about how you are doing in and for the organization.

PONDER: What do I really know of the character of God?

Am I cherishing and growing my relationship as a believer with Jesus my Lord and Savior?

How can I encourage my team to do this as well?

Other thoughts:

Now APPLY.

31. Documentation #1

It is vital that your organization document its activities and decisions. Early in the organization, I kept much of the important information in my head. I was good at that. Then came the time when our ministry began to grow, and we had a joke that what someone needed to know was *in Cinny's head*. It was funny but serious as well.

It is not healthy for an organization to revolve around one leader.

If I went off to Katmandu tomorrow, what would happen to the ministry? Write down all important information, make good notes, form a volunteer handbook, form a staff handbook, and design an office operations checklist. The Board is required by law to keep minutes and agendas in the records of the regular Board meetings. The discussion points and decisions regarding the operations and growth of the ministry are documented. There is always much to do. Take the time to put what is *in your head* on paper. If writing feels too time consuming, capture it on electronic text or talk it out to someone who will type up your thoughts. As a startup, task one person with the recording of information, progress made, and action taken. You are capturing history in the making.

PONDER: If I became incapacitated, how healthy would the ministry be without me?

What do we all take for granted that is not written down about how the organization operates?

What documentation is vital to capture for the organization to grow?

Other thoughts:

Now APPLY.

32. Documentation #2

Have you ever had a conversation with a friend or family member only to be told "You never said that"? I admit that there are times when I think I have communicated something, but in actuality did not. It is a good practice to verify the details of interactions you have with staff, leadership, donors, and others with an email or written note. This validates the conversation took place, and it offers a process for clarification. It also provides a tool for accountability regarding any next steps and who is responsible for what, when, and how. If there is a conflict, then this is a very concrete tool to use as a reference. A written record prevents the stereotypical *he said, she said...* and no resolution. This has been important after board, leadership, staff, and director meetings to keep us all moving in the same direction toward the mission of the ministry.

Yes, it takes time. Yes, it has to be filed somewhere (filing is NOT one of my strengths). But

documentation is irrefutable evidence.

Here is one example of a documentation process.

When a potential volunteer applies for training, we meet with them face to face. They bring a completed application to review with a staff member. We provide a copy of the training class calendar, a copy of the ministry's statement of faith, and a contract that outlines what they may expect from volunteering and what we expect from them as a volunteer. This clearly states the number of volunteer hours they will give in lieu of full payment for the training received.

The vast majority of the volunteers not only complete their hours but continue on to serve for years. They are fantastic! A few drop out of view quickly. We attempt verbal communication, and then email communication to express concern, offering support and opportunities to serve to complete their contractual agreement with us. If there is no response, then a letter with a copy of the signed contract is mailed with an invoice for the full training cost. This provides documented accountability they need to consider. Does this make us sound like tough guys? We have corporate boundaries and that includes documentation at all levels of the organization. Clear communication coupled with written support needs no clarification.

PONDER: When am I too soft in my expectations of volunteers or staff?

What documentation needs to be put in place for accountability to ensure the mission of the ministry moves forward?

How does this need to be communicated within our agency community?

Other ideas:

Now APPLY.

33. Do Not Cast Pearls Before Swine

It is interesting to see who values an organization and who does not. There are movers and shakers in any town. "You should go see "so and so." "I just know he will want to hear about this." "Try to get a meeting with—. It will be good for your credibility."

When in these face-to-face opportunities, I can sense within a short amount of time, whether or not the door is open to relate about the successes of the ministry. It is interesting to be talking while at the same time knowing you are being examined. Often I sense their agenda is more about being able to say they met me than it is about understanding the work we do. Their agenda is not the same as mine. I don't waste my time, theirs or my ministry's. Move quickly to make the conversation '-all about them-.' Learn what you can then go back to work.

Beware of bending the knee to get the approval of man. Respect everyone, but do not waste your time to gain blessings of the world. Focus on the mission God has called you.

The success of the ministry will draw interest, not because you sought it, but because it is earned.

PONDER: When have I been in a meeting and known it was not going to be a fruitful use of my time?

How did I handle it? Did I forgive the person for being *'that person'*?

Do I spend time working the *'network'*? How much and for what point?

Other thoughts:

Now **APPLY.**

34. *Donor Levels: Level The Field When You Can*

Whether the gift is $5 or $500, it is invaluable. All gifts are given because the donor wants to see the ministry continue and grow. Every single volunteer receives a thank you letter as well as touch points through newsletters and invitations.

    I Intentionally do not list donation amounts. All give out of their hard work and carefully saved funds to further the healing of women and their families by our great Lord. Yes, the big gifts are huge for us. They impact whether we have staff, can open more sites, or purchase a new computer. Yet I will never look askance at a donation of lesser denomination. We wouldn't be where we are without the regular gifts of $25 that come monthly. We wouldn't have inviting counseling sites without those who bring toilet paper, individually wrapped candy, and bottled water.

    Equally important is the time given by all the volunteers. I cannot even begin to capture the impact they make on hundreds of lives over the years. Every single person receives recognition and appreciation at the annual *Volunteer Appreciation Day*. We list all the volunteers in reports shared with the greater community.

I praise God for each and every one of the staff, the volunteers and the investors: those who gave seed money to purchase furniture and a copier when we began in 2004 and those who provide the matching gift challenges each spring. I praise God for paper towels and fresh white board markers. The expansiveness of their hearts is immeasurable.

PONDER: How do I recognize all who give to the ministry?

How can we foster a culture of appreciation for all time, all talents, and all treasures brought to us?

Other idea:

Now APPLY.

35. Don't Assume Anything

It has been my pleasure to attend many and varied fund-raisers, church worship services, and celebration events.. But I had to learn my cultural history is not the same as others. Just because I know how to do something does not mean everyone else does. I must enjoin others in how I would like something to be set up. I also need to learn that there are many different ways to accomplish the same goal.

Articulation of expectations is key. With this there is no need to fear talking down to someone. There is time for discussion with questions raised in a learning environment.

Of great importance is the 'what if' part of teaching.

This is a way to bring up questions a staff member or volunteer may have but isn't comfortable acknowledging they don't already know what to do or how to do it.

For example, we train our volunteers and staff not to acknowledge whether or not a specific person is in one of our programs. So what does that look like for someone answering the telephones? What if someone calls and says they are the client's child's school and need to get a message to the client? The training group discusses the best practice. The Trainer then states best answer. Another example: On the intake form for new clients it states that our organization does not provide childcare and not to bring children to appointments. What if someone brings her children with her? The scenario is addressed in the training class and also at the on-site orientation for volunteers. The Trainer or Staff then presents the best way to handle this.

PONDER: About what topics do I assume the staff and volunteers know that which I know?

What processes are in place or need to be put in place to teach and review best practices?

How can we do a better job of training and allowing for questions on how and why something is done a certain way?

Other thoughts:

Now APPLY.

36. *Don't Be An Agist*

As time has gone on, there are many volunteers and staff who are younger than I am. In relating to them I can go one of three ways. I can:

1. act like I know everything because I am older and expect blind obedience.
2. be nervous and point out I am older and forgetful and don't know anything like the young'uns do.
3. respect everyone including myself for the gathered knowledge of my life as well as what each person brings to the ministry regardless of age.

Yes, I do know quite a bit, but it is only because I have been at this business longer than some others. Each person, led by God, can accumulate knowledge and experience while blending their God-wired personhood into the experience.

I am getting older. I can still run circles around many, but I do not have as much energy as I used to. So I just acknowledge my limits and adjust accordingly without making a big deal out of it. Best practice is to welcome all—explore the vast and the minute. It will make each and all of us better.

PONDER: When do I, out of insecurity, raise myself above others?

When do I, out of insecurity, belittle myself to others?

Is ageism evident in the ministry's culture?

How can it be changed or prevented?

Other ideas:

Now APPLY.

37. Don't Be Sexist

There are ministries serving either men or women exclusively. A couple of thoughts about this. Please exchange men or women depending on your place of work. Also if both men and women receive care, these still apply to all.

1. Do not bash the opposite sex. Everyone has stories of being wronged by another, but don't allow the organization to be known as gender-haters or

worse. Choose language that elevates others. I have the expectation of who they can be, even if they aren't acting that way at the time.

2. Recognize that every woman knows at least one man. A pastor, spouse, son, brother, uncle, friend. As she gains strength through your business, it will impact everyone including the males in her sphere of influence. Therefore, uphold expectations for all, even the men in her life, to be raised up as she is raised through her focus on God and the help she receives.

3. The opposite sex—on site, on the Board? There are many with talents that we need in our organization. Therefore, we have gentlemen who serve as a graphic designer, as a photographer for events, and on the Board of Directors. Indirect service by these awesome gentlemen directly impacts our performance. They are wonderful contributors to what we do.

4. Being in an office many hours a day, invites conversations about family, etc. A bit of joking takes place. Yet it is important that no ministry denigrate the opposite sex. If your office is a blend or all male, do not denigrate women. If you are around me, you will always hear me refer to men as *gentlemen*. This is intentional so as to raise expectations that these men can be respected men of God, reaching toward the standard God places before them.

How to address the women? *'Ladies'* sounds condescending, *'girls'* is even worse. I prefer *women*. It is crisp and simple. We are women of God, wives, daughters, sisters, mothers, friends, and coworkers for Christ.

The law is exact on this topic: sexual discrimination is illegal.

Protect the image of God in each person, regardless of gender.

PONDER: How does our culture at the ministry portray members of the opposite sex?

Is there man or woman bashing in our organization?

Are bawdy jokes passed through emails to staff and volunteers?

How can the ministry elevate respect for one for another?

Other thoughts:

Now APPLY.

38. Don't Blame Me If You Don't Tell Me

Have you ever been in a conversation where the other person starts naming people and talking as if you two just spoke, yet you have no idea what the heck they are talking about? I appreciate that my companion thinks I can mind-read, but that is not a gift of mine. This is similar to ministry work. Others *assume* as a leader I know everything about every volunteer, client, issue, and more. If there is a problem that hasn't been addressed, it is presumed I am a bad leader even though I am not aware of the problem.

How can I address something if I do not know about it? Make sure you have communicated clearly and respectfully how your team is expected to handle a concern they have with you as the leader or with each other. All of us must refrain from emotionally and defensively confronting. We are human and do not respond well to emotional combat. I remind my team I do not know everything, and to please refrain from blaming me until I have been informed of the problem. I can't be blamed if I am unaware. Politicians and indicted corporate heads may plead ignorance, but I see that as an excuse used by many. I take very seriously any concern and welcome discussion. Also *talking around* it or murmuring is unbiblical.

A leader should be open to respectful questions.

As a leader, I request the information and time to ponder in order to formulate a solution. Then I do reply. The individual who brought the concern must prayerfully decide if they can live with how the ministry will move forward on that issue or not. If not, then God's blessings as He calls them to serve in another capacity.

At home, I received a call, "Are you coming?" Anyone who gets this type of call knows it really is saying "Where are you? You are supposed to be here." Apparently, a meeting was about to begin at the ministry and I was expected to attend. I had no knowledge of the meeting. Fortunately, I was able to arrive within ten minutes of the start. I put on my diplomacy hat, participated and the meeting went well. Afterwards, I apologized for being late and asked what method was used to notify me of the meeting. I did not assume someone had acted incorrectly – yet. Three missteps had happened: 1. Two leaders assumed the other had told me, 2. An inoperative email had been used to send me the minutes with next meeting times, 3. They thought I was always on site so would 'just know.' Corrections were made and we moved on.

As a leader it is not easy to balance what I know, what I am expected to know, and what I am responsible to know.

Harsh? No, this is straight talk. There will not be agreement all the time on all things. Yet as a leader I will lead. Others have the freedom of will to determine their walk with God at this ministry or not. Just do not blame the leader or the ministry.

PONDER: As a leader, am I receptive to challenges to my leadership?

Do I reply with respect or conveniently forget the uncomfortable question?

Do I as a leader allow murmuring? How do I, my staff, and my Board address this? Is the process written down so everyone knows how to bring a concern to leadership?

How have I behaved when I have a complaint? Have I respectfully taken it to the leader or talked behind his back?

Other thoughts:

Now APPLY.

39. Don't Compare

We all do it. We compare hair, cars, bodies, watches, shoes, what and how each other eats; the church you attend, the prayers you say... it is endless. And now with all the social media, we are either stalking others to see what their lives are like, or posting like a maniac to justify how good our own lives are.

We do it with ministries as well. I have had to incorporate the Bible verse: laugh and cry with other organizations (Ecclesiastes 3:1, 4). When another ministry has great mailings or advertises a great-sounding event with a super speaker or posts the success of something, it is easy to feel insecure about what our organization is attempting. It is easy to feel lesser than if I only look at the successes of other ministries and forget to focus on how lavishly God has been guiding and providing for us. God also has blessed the organization faithfully. There has been steady growth each year coupled with trials. I must, absolutely MUST, make sure that how we present information for praise, brings praise of the Lord and does not bring praise of us, either by elevating the ministry or devaluing others.

We are NOT in a competition—we are in this together.

If another ministry is doing well, be supportive, not jealous. If another is struggling, be caring, not gloating.

PONDER: How do I feel when I hear about the success of another ministry?

What do I think when I hear about the struggles of another ministry?

How do I reply when either a success or a struggle is shared with me? Am I caring or dismissive?

How can our ministry support ministry friends during successes and during struggles?

Other thoughts:

Now APPLY.

40. Don't Compromise For A Buck

The most critical document in the formation of a ministry is the Statement of Faith. This is not a compilation of your and the Board's beliefs. It is what God says regarding who He is, what He does, and how the ministry will operate. It sets the tone for all points forward.

Two other critical declarations are the Mission Statement and Vision Statement. Everything that is done flows back to seeing the Mission fulfilled and the Vision complete. Any challenge, direct or indirect, must be filtered through these documents.

Recently the Board of Directors, with additional advisors, updated the language of the aforementioned documents. Keeping with our behavior of transparency, all who are staff, Board, or active volunteers were sent copies with a request for a response noting if they concurred, desired to dialogue about the changes, or at this time wished to serve God in a different way. Any time there is change, some will rotate out of the ministry. It is natural. Two volunteers felt it was time to rotate to inactive status, and two desired to talk about the updates with a Board member and me. The sharing was deep and good. Several prayer team volunteers shared they were either not being active in their prayer support or were not comfortable with the changes. All were thankful for what God is doing at the Eve Center but stated they were headed in other directions.

Two other individuals heading in a different direction were significant donors. I was aware that any change of the status quo could bring shifts in personnel and financial support. Even with the clearest communication, the shift happens. Was keeping the donors and volunteers more important than the updated language? Not to us. Yet this can be a stumbling point for others who depend on the funders and the volunteers.

Always and in all ways stay the course as God shows you.

Be sure to thank and bless those who chose to move on to another church, business, or ministry. Do not compromise for the buck – in donated time or financial gift.

PONDER: Who is the head of your ministry: God or the dollar?

Has the Board reviewed the Mission Statement, the Vision Statement, and Statement of Faith to insure each has the necessary language to communicate allegiance to God and His inerrant Word, the Bible?

What self-awareness do I need to be attune to compromise?

Other thoughts:

Now APPLY:

41. Don't Cook The Books

"The campaign donor won't know because they aren't aware of the bookkeeping in the organization. We will just know internally." This statement was a fork in the road for me. The ministry is blessed by two investors who provide the matching funds for a campaign to encourage donations for the summer months. Another donor who had committed to give regularly toward a specific project wanted to know if we would count their regular monthly donation toward the match. Sure, we could present that any funds that came in during the campaign months would count toward the goal. But we had not communicated that to the matching campaign donors, nor in the campaign language to our broader community. The point of the annual campaign is to bring in new, extra, additional funds above what is currently coming through regular donors. Most important is this could be construed as ambiguous accounting. What was the correct way to account for the funds? Either the funds were to be listed toward program support or toward the project.

I offered the regular donor two choices: to extend their support of the project an extra month and have this month's gift count toward the matching campaign, or leave it as supporting the project selected before the campaign announcement. I carefully worded this—each and every donor is valuable no matter the size of the gift. Their desire to see the ministry grow is commendable. It is my role to ensure the ethics are always excellent. Always and in all ways keep all aspects of the ministry on the high road. As the leader, I set the tone. The Highest Board President (God) will require a report. Besides being wrong, it is illegal.

PONDER: Are there any *white lies* around your organization's fund raiser bookkeeping?

Am I prepared to answer a question like the one in the example above at my ministry?

What ways can I, as the leader, raise the bar regarding our finances to be better than what is normative in society?

Other thoughts:

Now APPLY.

42. Don't Drown Others In Your Enthusiasm

Years of prayer, time, and energy have been put into the ministry. We witness lives changing, healing, and growing every day. I can hardly contain the joy and the fullness of my soul. I want everyone to grasp it and come be a part of it. If you haven't guessed, I have more than the "glass half full" personality. I am the "glass full to overflowing." I know I can be a bit intense (Do I hear a loud *yea!* from those reading who know me?), when I tell about God and the ministry. My intent is pure, yet my enthusiasm can drown the very people I wish to hear the miracles and more.

It is important to temper my passion to give others room to breathe.

What to do with all my zeal? God made me full-to-overflowing, so I had to find those who can take the energetic (almost hyper) download of what I wish to share. This audience loves me and can handle the intensity. Once I have released all my hot air, I breathe and dial it down so that then, when I share, it is honoring and doesn't knock over the glasses of others—spilling their living water because I wasn't listening to their God-walk stories. When we feel heard, only then can we listen.

As the Founder and the one who had the original vision, I can have corrupted thoughts. One thought is that everyone should be as passionate about the ministry as I am. Everyone should make time to complete all the tasks, projects and programs that need attention for my organization to be a success. I had to learn that others have lives, and to encourage them to have good boundaries to protect their priorities. As a leader it is important not to be the only one to speak. If I am always presenting, there is no room for others to be heard. The unspoken message to others is they aren't needed because the leader seems to take care of everything. Accurate? Maybe! Healthy for the ministry? No! Praise God He made me aware that if I was not careful I would drown those around me; drown out what they had to offer in word and deed. I would be flushing away wisdom, joy and the opportunity to learn from other wise women and men.

PONDER: Do I intentionally make room in conversations and meetings for others to participate?

Do I always need to be the focal point of others?

Am I too quiet? Do I wait to be asked for my thoughts or am I willing to step up as a leader to offer counsel and direction?

How can I appreciate those who are different than me without changing who I am?

How can I be a better listener?

How do I engage others so I learn how to be a better leader?

Other ideas:

Now APPLY.

43. *Don't Expect Too Much*

Don't expect the Church to support your ministry. It has enough of its own agenda items to cover. Many churches struggle to meet their own bills much less support extra mission organizations. Our ministry is blessed by several churches that do give to our mission. Yet, it is a fallacy to assume funding will come primarily through the Church.

What you can do is support the Church. Reach out and pray for any pastors, ministers, or priests in a five-mile radius. Send a card of support. The church is a consumer: what can your staff and volunteers, offer the church's members and leaders? How can you be a part of their body instead of wanting the church to be a part of yours? When you bless them, God in turn will bring you favor from sources you could not dream up.

PONDER: What churches are in our five-mile radius?

What way can we make a regular practice at our ministry of supporting the Church?

Other ideas:

Now APPLY.

44. Don't Hide From What You Don't Know

Have you ever wanted to close your eyes, put your fingers in your ears and say "La, la, la…" to avoid something? I have. Sometimes, things seemed insurmountable as the ministry has grown. The things that are not naturally in my wheelhouse intimidate me—yes me, the strong extrovert.

    Struggling with handling criticism, I would rather just hide from what I don't know or don't want to deal with. There is so much to learn, that at times, it is hard to focus where to start. Stinking thinking says if I just ignore what I don't know, maybe it won't matter. Mental conversations follow: "I can't, I don't want to, Why me? Why now?" This then builds a freeze-response in me, and I don't do anything. This works for a time. But eventually our good, kind leader, God, taps me on the shoulder and points to it. I can't hide. So I humbly cry and tell Him I don't know how… After I put the burden down at the foot of His throne, I am free to focus on His call, His direction. Intimidation recedes. And I break into praise, "Oh God! You are so good to me. Praise You Wonderful God who does not punish me, or fault me. Instead You draw me forward." Then I can freely tell others what I need because my current skill set is limited.

It is Okay to be intimidated. It is a HUGE thing God is doing.

    I cannot know everything. I do not know everything. I must not think that I should know everything. No one does! I Praise God that He is in charge on the ride of my life. I am okay. He will bring others who do know what I do not. I will continue to learn. It is all good!

PONDER: What freezes me and keeps me from doing the work of the ministry?

How do I handle feeling inadequate?

How can I articulate the need clearly so others will step forward to fill in the gaps?

Other thoughts:

Now APPLY.

45. Don't Live In The Margins

The demands of leadership on our time are crushing. It is vital to establish a regimen of behavior. Protect your sleep. Eat properly. Invest in your family. Guard time with God DAILY.

Even with these guidelines, it is sooo easy to break the boundaries. When asked to do something, "Sure" is often my reply. One because it would be fun; second, you asked me; third, I might feel I can't say no… More than anything else, as a fourth answer, I often think, sure—I can fit this in. This automatic response needs to be stopped.

If you are like me, I am then tired, and resentful. My family makes it known their needs aren't being met. I find myself squeezed into the narrow margins of life. What kind of an example am I as a leader if I am tired and stressed, accusing others of not helping me or understanding all I have to do?

Instead of living foundationally—guarding my structure, making thoughtful, prayerful decisions about my time and energy, I am living in the margin.

This may be your normal. But it isn't normal or healthy. So step back, finish what you have committed to. Do not accept any more responsibilities until you return to the throne room and ask your big boss (God), what His priorities are. You will sleep, eat, exercise, worship, relate, and lead from a better place.

If you do need to take on extra responsibilities, make sure it is an exception and not the rule for your life.

PONDER: Am I living in the margins?

In what ways?

What do I need to do to stop this?

What are my reasons for taking on more than I can handle?

How can I prevent this?

Other thoughts

Now APPLY.

46. Don't Make The Job Fit The Person. What Is Best For The Organization?

When the Eve Center was small, we structured what we did around the person. Hours matched when we could be there. We talked much, shared a lot, and were close personally. We each knew what needed to be done, so we pitched in and got it done. This works well at the cottage ministry level. We would shift things around to fit our needs. We were small enough to check on each other and share in the tasks at hand.

As we grew, it had to change. God has called many. Therefore, communicating, relating, and ensuring we are focused forward required new procedures be put in place. As each person completes the basic training required to volunteer, they have has the opportunity to engage in many different ways. We fit them into a place that matches the mission of the ministry with the talents they exhibit. Originally relationships were all lateral: one for all and all for one – a tight group. Now growth requires a vertical organizational chart. All consistent communication and teaching from the staff, seasoned volunteers and key leadership reach the massive group of volunteers. Relationships are still sister-to-sister as well as mentor or seasoned volunteer or staff to others. We are strongly woven together. This required restructuring the organization

Delegation is a skill that can be learned. Begin with your team talking about how the ministry is going. Use the SWOT (Strength Weakness Opportunity Threat) tool to flush out what are the priorities. Then assign who will own the steps for change and improvement.

Assign each person who is a part of your ministry to a staff person or key leader. The staff or key leader will keep an eye on their group. Mentoring, loving, praying for – these can be identified roles for the staff or key leaders. Retention will be high. Being a part of something not just giving, builds community.

PONDER: What does our organization flow chart look like?

Is it stronger at one end or the other?

What intentional changes are needed to engage more people?

What do I as a leader need to let go of and allow others to take the lead?

Other thoughts:

Now APPLY.

47. Don't Undercut Someone At Their Own Event

As a leader I am invited to as many functions as I choose to attend. Some are informative seminars, while others are fund-raisers for one charity or another. When I attend, I am either a general supporter, a guest of a supporter, or attending as a representative of my organization. Regardless, I am always aware that I am there to support the hosting organization. When asked what I do or introduced by my affiliation with Eve Center, I share BRIEFLY then focus back to how the others know about the hosting organization. It is not the time to network and solicit support for my cause. We have had events where it is obvious that others are in attendance purely for selfish motives.

We must support one another and not be fishing in another's pond.

Being enthusiastic is one thing. But stop talking after 30 seconds about you and yours and uplift the hard workers of the ministry at hand. If I trust God completely, then I have no need to take from others what is not mine in the first place.

PONDER: How have I unconsciously fished in another's pond?

Do I trust God to supply all my ministry's needs?

What is my motive when I attend another ministry's functions?

How can I actively appreciate other's work?

Other thoughts that kicked up considering this topic:

Now APPLY.

48. *Dress For Respect Not For Effect*

Too casual, too revealing... long-sleeved shirt only... what is the proper dress for your volunteers and staff? Generations and cultures have different guidelines for what is acceptable. When our youngest child was applying for employment during high school, I shared an observation. Most supervisors and bosses are over the age of thirty. They tuck their shirts in or wear an ensemble: a coordinated look of shirt and pants with appropriate accessories. So dress to impress. As Christians and as leaders we dress to respect the recipient —the one who you will be meeting and greeting in your organization. It is not to show off one's status.

It is important to draft guidelines that are acceptable to the various consumers: volunteers and clients. My rule is "just not jeans." Be a step above home casual. Nothing too short (when you sit your thighs are not bare). Nothing that shows cleavage. I find it difficult to maintain eye contact while a woman's chest is distractingly apparent. Gentlemen, don't come dressed in wrinkles. It is not attractive. Dirty, old shoes get you nowhere. Belt – wear one. My point? Dress to respect the person with whom you are meeting. Period.

What one wears reflects how they think of themselves. Do you think of yourself as loved, valuable, attractive, and worth knowing? Or do you dress to blend into the shadows? A pop of color or an attractive cut to a shirt is just good style. Being *out there* in your choices can draw negative attention to yourself in one of two ways, you can't be taken seriously because you look silly, or you couldn't possibly understand the observer. Don't be beige and boring, I'm not saying that. Strike a balance that shows color, and your personality while respecting that the customer, investor, or coworker is *'looking'* at you.

PONDER: How do I present myself as a leader at work? Am I modeling leadership in appearance?

Do I dress as someone to be respected, who respects themselves?

Am I underdressed to *'fit in'*?

What is the dress code at the ministry?

Is it in writing?

Other ideas:

Now APPLY.

49. Empty The Trash

Jesus washed the feet of disciples. If he could do that, I can empty the trash. I do not expect a volunteer or staff person to do what I will not do. Show that every aspect of the ministry is important:

1. It is not below me to swab a toilet or empty the staff refrigerator.
2. For those who may assume these tasks, I must show it is important enough that I am willing to do it.
3. I value everything, large and small, that is part of the organization. Just as the church is the body, so is each piece of our place. It all counts in God's economy.
4. Gladly accept every donation regardless of actual usefulness

Do not be one of those leaders who expects to have servant-staff/leader hierarchy.

Respect is one thing. Veneration is absolutely inappropriate. So work and model value in each task and each person.

PONDER: Do I at times think more highly of myself than I should?

When was the last time I attended to the physical needs of the ministry?

Do I allow others to think I am so important I couldn't possibly attend to something as mundane as trash?

When have I thanked those who do clean our office?

Other thoughts that kicked up considering this topic:

Now APPLY.

50. Engaging The Quiet Ones

United States culture values an extrovert more than an introvert. There are many loud mouths with opinions on everything. It is a noisy world. Be a wise leader. Silence your brain/mouth and move to engagement. Instead of answering every question yourself, respond with a question. Ask the inquirer or others present: "What do you suggest?" Then pause for them to think and reply.

Approach the quieter ones and ask for their thoughts about an issue. These individuals may have a ready reply or need some time to formulate a thoughtful response. Allow for this. It will be well worth it. This shows you value their wisdom, by taking the time to seek them out, and being willing to wait for an answer. Some are quiet because they:

1. Don't think you want their ideas.
2. Don't think well on the spot.
3. Haven't had a leader ask before.

This will grow them. This shows others you want everyone's insights. It is good for you to breathe and listen. You will be wiser for it.

PONDER: Do I have a ready answer for everything?

How can I redirect a question posed to me to another allowing more inclusion in discussions?

What do I truly think of someone who is quiet? (This is for the extroverts).

What do I truly think of someone who is very talkative? (This is for the introverts).

Other ideas:

Now APPLY.

51. *Every Day Matters—The Dash*

What does every tombstone have in common in a cemetery? It is the dash mark between the birth and death dates. That little line represents your life on earth. It seems so small, but it is so valuable to the Lord.

What are you doing with your dash? Are you distracted? Are you bogged down in minutiae of others' needs? Are you being pulled and pushed in every direction by the duties of your life and love? It may be time to take a break and go spend time with God. Clear your head and refocus on what He is saying. Reprioritize and delegate to others things that will further the mission but are not for you to do. If you only had thirty days left, what are the musts for your ministry? What are the musts of your position in leadership? Are you trying to do others' dashes?

Most leaders of nonprofits work many more hours than they are paid—many more. And beyond their actual presence at the business office, there is all the think-time and prayer-time outside regular hours. There comes a time for any leader to assess their role. A leader's job description must be updated as the ministry grows. Regular strategic planning involves priority setting for programs, human resources and fund development. The dash of each person within the ministry needs ongoing evaluation and reordering. STOP. God's holy name is I AM. It is not 'I was' nor 'I will be.' Today delegate the 80% of your job that others can do. Focus on the 10% you can train others do to and delegate. Then enjoy attending to the 10% ONLY YOU can do in ways only God gave you.

PONDER: Considering my ministry dash, what needs evaluation?

Is there a business development plan in our ministry?

Is my team receiving reviews in a timely fashion?

Other thoughts:

Now APPLY.

52. *Everyone Wants A Piece Of The Action*

Capitalism is defined as "an economic system based on private ownership of the means of production and their operation for profit" (https://en.wikipedia.org/wiki/Capitalism) 5-26-16). The United States is a wonderful country in which to start and extend businesses. We receive inquiries from small and large businesses that desire to partner with the Eve Center with promises to grow our fund base or bring more clients. Some requests come as 800-number cold calls. Those are easy to reply to: "No thank you." It is the requests from small business owners and start-ups, volunteers or their spouses and children that are more emotionally charged. Many of the ideas they bring are wonderful. Yet we cannot commit. Our vision is established. Our mission is clear.

There are reasons we stick to what we are doing currently. To prevent playing favorites we stay focused on the fund development plan established by the Fund Development Committee of the Board. Even for those who will host an event and donate back a percentage of the profits, we do not release our database nor send out invitations to attend the fundraisers of other organizations. It confuses our message and dilutes the participation in our agency-specific events. It is not our role to market another's business. However, when cash sponsorships are given to the Eve Center, there is a communicated agreement specifying what support will be received in return for the donation.

We've also been asked to consider adding nutrition groups or yoga or other good programs. We stick to the Mission. If the great new program does not line up with it, we must refuse. If we were to grab onto all these great ideas, we would dilute what we do well. I salute everyone who dreams big with ideas galore. Keep asking, just know we may not add your vision into our mission.

PONDER: How do I respond to inquiries from sales persons and staff about new opportunities at the ministry?

Have I been distracted by *'new'* and wandered off from the mission?

Has the Board prepared and reviewed the budget with balance sheets monthly?

Other thoughts:

Now APPLY.

53. *Expense Generous, Income Conservative*

In preparing the annual budget, do not underestimate the costs to provide the programs of your mission. It takes far more than you may realize. It is wonderful to come in under budget. While you know your mission is God-given and everyone should invest in it, raising funds is not easy. Therefore, be conservative about what funds will be generated. It is not automatic. If you have not had the privilege of raising funds, have high respect for those who do and be very grateful for the gifts received. To build a budget, ask other similar ministries about their costs. Estimate costs when necessary. As soon as actual expenses can be reported, make an updated budget. Compare actual income to what is projected in the budget. Using this format will ease your anxiety about money. It will be realistic, something attainable, not pie in the sky, something unattainable.

PONDER: Do I make promises about fundraising? Do I paint an unrealistic picture?

Am I engaged in seeking financial gifts or do I leave it to others?

Is my Board active in raising enough to sustain the ministry?

What needs to change?

Other thoughts:

Now APPLY.

54. Financial Road Rash

There is no way to prepare for the unforeseen. Sometimes it is an expense that could not be predicted. For us it was a lack of planning for growth when the ministry began. I did not know to plan for financial rainy days. Individuals and families are told to keep six months of reserve in case of illness or loss of income. Our problem was we grew faster than the budget. We were used to living day to day. There came a season where it was touch and go. We had to reach out specifically to investors to give extra gifts to carry us through. God was and is so good. We have always paid all bills in full and on time. But that nine months of financially grinding along the concrete, taught us to plan. Now we watch our funds and purposefully bank three months or more of expenses in case of lower than expected income. Now with wisdom, we have proper budgeting and savings in place.

There are additional ways to avoid financial road rash:

FROM CLOUDS TO CONCRETE

1. Do not take on projects that cannot be sustained in the future.
2. Do not spend funds on fancy print materials.
3. **Focus on what God told you to do and stay lean.**
4. **Never casually say God will take care of it. He is not a genie in a bottle called upon to fix what you messed up.**
5. Do not extend the debt. Pay it off quickly.
6. You may learn a hard financial road rash lesson. If you do experience this, determine exactly what must happen to protect the investment of your donors.

Continue to communicate the success of the programs that are operating. Always '*look up*' to God, not down at the asphalt. It is important to remember why we are all here: remember the mission of the ministry.

PONDER: Has our ministry ever been strapped for funds?

How did the Board and I handle it?

What are the financial goals and what protections are in place to protect the ministry?

What needs to change?

Other thoughts:

Now APPLY.

55. Flooding

There is no way around this tough topic. At some point you will have someone who you truly do not like within the ministry. Most of the time *out of sight, out of mind* is how I tried to manage the struggle. If I don't have to interact with the person, then I don't have to confront my feelings of dislike. Yet there are times when the mind gets going.

Thoughts of *how that person upsets me* can fill the mind even when I am not at work or not with that person. It is called flooding. The mere thought of that person triggers a flood of emotions that are overwhelming. This causes emotional stress and disturbs my beliefs, thoughts, and behavior. When this is happening, you are giving this person too much power. If the source of flooding is a person within the ministry, it is best to seek outside counsel. This will prevent damaging the flood-provoking person by choosing not to download your distress in front of other ministry associates.

Review what is reality and what is your mental fantasy/nightmare. Is there real cause for alarm? Is there a narcissistic personality within your organization or are you an alpha leader feeling threatened by another strong person?

Remember, no one can change another person; you can only change yourself.

So seek ways to deal with this for yourself and for the betterment of the organization. It is a growth opportunity for the other person as well.

PONDER: Is there someone I avoid in the ministry? Why?

On a scale of 1 to 10, (10 being most severe) how distressed am I because of this person?

What attempts have been made between the two of you to find common ground?

Who can I talk to about this? Make the appointment.

Can I remain in the ministry if this person is also there?

Other ideas:

Now APPLY.

56. *Four Main Food Groups*

When I am stressed, not focused, or just feeling rebellious, I eat "*Cinny's four main food groups*": Salt, Sugar, Fat and Caffeine. While these may taste great, they are not the best nutritionally. Lead by example: eat your fruits and veggies. Enjoy nuts and drink lots of water. Make chocolate or Doritos a nice extra, but not your main entrée. You will sleep better, feel better, and look better—glowing skin and all that!

PONDER: Am I eating for longevity or a short life time?

Am I rewarding myself with sweets every day?

Here is my plan to include more glasses of water each day:

Other thoughts:

Now APPLY.

57. Gate Crashers: Boundaries

These are folks who want me to do what they want and do it right now. I don't think they know how much time is involved in leading a nonprofit.

These individuals are full of ideas and enthusiasm, but don't listen well. If already involved in the ministry, they feel the rules do not apply to them. They crash my staff's gates. They demand their way by breaching the ministry walls on the way to conquering the world. How does one reign in these wild characters?

1. Make sure you have set up a structure so there is no doubt about the process in place and what is expected in terms of bringing concerns and ideas to the leadership.
2. Make sure you have communicated to your leaders and the others in your ministry community that the leaders, both volunteer and staff, have the authority to hear and determine next steps regarding any new request to add or amend what the ministry does and how it is done.
3. Direct the gate crasher back to the person they are to report to if they have breached the wall by crashing your gate.

The gate crasher is usually a charmer, "While I could have talked to—, I know you are the one who would know best what to do" or "I wasn't sure you knew what was going on so, I thought I should get your thoughts on this." This is undermining and disrespectful to you as a leader and to the team. As mentioned, direct the person back to the proper channel. If that person in authority does not have the answer, they, not the gate crasher, can talk with you. This encourages growth in your team and keeps the structure intact.

Either the gate crasher will become dissatisfied and leave the ministry, or they will work within the structure of your organization, by settling in and adhering to the boundaries. These two outcomes are good. A third outcome signals a need for intervention.

The gate crasher may not only go around the proper person and you. They may approach another person on the team. Stirring the pot like this is harmful, time-consuming, confusing, and brings more attention to the gate crasher. A swiftly scheduled face to face by the proper person is indicated. Authority must be respected. If another infraction occurs, then determine who will need to be present at the next meeting. Document all of this, whether it concerns a staff person, volunteer, Board member, or other entity. There are times when we have had to address this kind of concern. Most often it is a lack of understanding and simply a settling-in to respect structure. Our culture has so few healthy organizational structures. Build one and be one.

PONDER: Who are the gate crashers in my ministry?

How does my team handle these individuals?

Am I comfortable with being firm with a boundary breaker?

How can I set a structure for managing time takers?

Am I a boundary breaker?

Other thoughts:

Now APPLY.

58. Get Good Counsel

Every person you ask for advice will offer a different opinion. You will also find there are many people who feel threatened by the thought of another ministry that may be in any way similar to theirs. They can be reluctant to share their good ideas with you. Some have pat answers on what you should do. Even some in the Christian community will have pat answers for the way to do things. So it can be hard to find someone who will truthfully and genuinely give you good advice.

First, if you are a believer in Jesus Christ as Lord and Savior, spend time in prayer. Write down any ideas that come to mind during that time: such as someone to reach out to for counsel, something to research, an organization to meet with to hear their path of growth. Then thank God for the list. Now ask God what He wants you to learn and what questions to ask. Be obedient to follow through on this task list from God.

When contacting a person, attempt three times to connect. If that person doesn't respond, that lack of reply is on them. You have been obedient.

Seek two persons of differing backgrounds who are willing to consult with you every now and then. Do not expect these two to be available all the time. Unless this is a paid consultant, they are giving beyond their own commitments to assist you. When you do connect, respect their time. Be prepared with a brief outline of what you are doing and what you are seeking from this meeting. Ask, then shut up and listen. Take notes, ask clarifying questions, thank them and leave. Send a follow up email or written thank-you.

Work with each of those two to define what you need from them: emotional support, management support, community contacts, leader to leader mentoring. In other words, what will make the best of your contact time? Over thirteen years of ministry leadership, I have had four mentors; two with whom I am still in contact.

One mentor is a pastor who was of great assistance when I was struggling with difficult personalities in the ministry. A second advisor has helped me know my leadership strengths and weaknesses. A third has been a good community connection and support for me personally as a growing leader. The fourth is special: he has stood alongside for several years kindly, wisely and extremely patiently giving good counsel. Some I heard and did, other times I heard the good advice, but didn't get to it until years later. Know what you need and seek that out.

PONDER: Do I have a mentor?

What do I do when I need wise counsel?

Do I follow through with what they recommend?

Do I feel better about myself and my work after we meet?

If I do not, what needs to change?

Other thoughts:

Now APPLY.

59. *Give It Back To God*

There came a time in the progress of the ministry where I wondered, "Is this as good as it gets?" The ministry was doing well. It was stable financially, volunteers were being trained to counsel women so their lives are changed for the better, and credibility was good. My mind would ping out across the horizon and wonder, "Is this good enough, God?" Do I strive for more or was this as far as God was taking it? If this is it, then great! I was okay with that. Yet it was time to place it before the Lord.

So I brought Eve Center to the altar, giving it back to God. It is His after all. He called it into being and He provided me with enough equipping. He has called many to be a part of this mission. He brought it to this day. It was now up to Him to determine what was next. That was five years in.

God did not close the doors nor leave it as is. He did not even take the ministry from me, review it, and hand it back. Instead He blew it up—He renewed my passion. He brought affirmation to confirm we were to continue. He called more women to come for training and for care. He brought new board members. He has continued to place it on investor's hearts to give.

Be ready to give the gift of the ministry to the One who gave it in the first place.

Keep your grip loose.

PONDER: Have I reached a plateau in ministry?

What do I need to talk with God about?

Have I ever given this incredible gift of vision and ministry back to Him for further development?

Other thoughts:

Now APPLY.

60. *Glass Half Empty, Glass Half Full*

We are all wired differently. Consequently, we see situations differently. You probably know which style you are. If *glass half full*, you are more apt to see the positive and give grace generously. If you are *glass half empty*, you are good at seeing potential pitfalls and can point to risks ahead. Both are good traits to have but the two styles can cause tension in decision-making meetings. A person with a *Half full* glass desires to move ahead and considers the strengths of the ministry able to overcome any obstacles; going forward will be good for the mission. A person with a *Half empty* glass is perceptive and desires good planning, acknowledging threats are real and to overcome them, the ministry must grow carefully. This style brings many thoughtful questions and requires much assurance before consenting to change.

Both are right and both are wrong—if viewed separately. At this juncture, refer back to your mission, vision, and goals. Build unity by accord. Organize into facts what needs attention and what is a priority. This reduces the volume of concerns to priorities.

It keeps in check the fearless and gives peace to the hesitant.

It recognizes the good that is present and can build on this foundation. It also grows individuals into a team with respect for process and maintains focus for going forward. Value the wisdom of each whether your style or not.

PONDER: Which style am I, half-full or half-empty?

Do I have both styles on my team?

When has this been an issue for my team?

What steps can be put in place for strengthening the team?

Other thoughts:

Now APPLY.

61. *Go Eat Lunch*

In the 1980s I worked for Hamilton County Juvenile Court—adult jurisdiction. My position was Case Manager for Dependency, Neglect, and Abuse filings. Parents were being monitored to either reunite with their children who had been removed from the home or were at risk to lose custody. Nancy Reagan had declared war on child abuse so reports to police and child welfare agencies were skyrocketing. I was so new in the job. This was before computers. Everything was in the form of paper files. I was drowning. I was working through lunch, after hours, and on weekends. My wonderful supervisor called me into her office and taught me a life lesson. I have boiled it down to this:

The job will always be here, you won't. So go eat lunch.

The Bible tells us the poor and suffering will always be among us. We are to care for them. Because we are human, we must do what we can and then stop to restore ourselves to be of use the next day. In non-profit work, there are always clients to assist, staff needing mentoring, funds to be raised, papers to review, and communication to do. I only provide benefit if I am contributing in a healthy way. So I do eat lunch, and not at my desk.

PONDER: How have I let the cares of work get me off-balance?

How do I shake off the troubles of the world and ministry?

How do I recharge? When is the last time I did recharge, not just to half battery?

Who on my team is showing signs of low battery life?

Other thoughts:

Now APPLY.

62. *God First Always*

Do not forget that without God you would not be where you are. God works with you and in spite of you. He has endowed you with talents, and when you have bungled many things, God has disciplined you with life lessons. It is okay to be proud of what is happening at the ministry. You are doing great work. But never forget the source of it all. Any time you or the ministry is complimented, thank the giver and refer to our Lord. Gather several replies for your diplomacy toolbox: "Thank you. All that happens is due to God," "Thank you. Truly lives are being changed by what God is doing." "Thank you, we have been blessed beyond measure," "Thank you, I owe all I do to a loving God." It doesn't need to be a longwinded Oscar-length speech, just a simple acknowledgement.

PONDER: How do I handle a compliment?

Do I take all the praise, deflect it all to God, or appreciate the affirmation while recognizing our Lord?

How do I model this for others?

Other thoughts:

Now APPLY.

63. God First? Family First? Which Is It?

I did hear God's calling. I did and do respond.

Does this trump the responsibilities to my husband, to my children, to my parents? It is vital that you as a leader protect your relationship with your spouse and your children.

Do not let resentment towards God happen because your spouse or children think you favor your ministry over them.

Do not bring work home. Do not take calls from ministry during family time. I did at one time. I can remember taking calls in the evening and my children would be all over the place, jumping on beds, going for snacks they weren't to have, bickering. I just wanted to take a phone call, yet I was expecting them to be a part of *my* call, *my* ministry. It is not their call nor their ministry. So I changed the message on the phone: "If you are calling between six and nine p.m., we are having dinner, baths, bedtime. Leave a message and we will call you back." Then I turned the ringer off so I wasn't distracted.

Life certainly was calmer when I did that. I was focused on the children, and they could see by my actions I was there exclusively for them. In this virtual world, we contact each other when it is a good time for us, not necessarily for the receiver of our communications. I do tell everyone they can always call me. However, I also use the *do not disturb* function on my phone that prevents anyone not on my favorites list getting through at specific times.

God is my God, my all in all, my source of everything. He has gifted me with family. Two of my roles are wife and mother. Another role is in leadership. Keep them separate so no resentment grows.

Another caution is to not run away from home and the challenges there because you 'must serve God'. That is a fallacy. If you are dodging facing struggles in your marriage or how to nurture your children, you are not bringing glory to God. Go home! Your calling is no excuse to be weak in your personal life. It is a blatant slap to integrity. Be the same in public as in private.

PONDER: When have I expected my loved ones to be a part of my ministry?

How are my relationships? To what do I need to be attentive and change?

Other thoughts:

Now APPLY.

64. God Makes It Quite Clear

For two years we had a location that came about through a word from God. Driving down a bankrupt, beat-up main road through a neglected, poor area of Cincinnati, God said, "Who will care for these? They too are my children."

We opened a location in that area. Women's lives were touched but it became evident that the financial cost outweighed the realities that were needed to keep it open.

The Board met on a Saturday in August. In prayer we gave the location to God. We received clear direction that day: the plan for site development would now be Good NEWS: North, East, West and South with Central/HQ in the middle of the zone bounded by the interstate beltway. The small site under discussion did not fit this vision and would close. Due to our various personal calendars, we would complete the closing within a few weeks. Since there was furniture and items to be moved, internet/phone to cancel, volunteers and clients to notify—there was no rush. We wrapped up about 10:30 a.m.

By eight that evening the police had called us to the site. A robbery had taken place. The telephone bank cords were ripped from the wall. The computer, the large video/TV and DVD/VCR player as well as the bathroom and cleaning supplies were all stolen. The file cabinet with client files was beaten but not broken into. Being a very confidential ministry, we praised God that the most important items, the client's stories, were safe. The cabinet was so badly damaged it took my wielding a sledge hammer to get it open to retrieve the files.

We moved everything out the next day. We praised God no one was hurt. We praised God that He did tell us to get out—we just thought we could work through our human time schedule. We had asked God for His direction but didn't listen for His timing. Lesson learned.

PONDER: When have I heard from God and then stalled in disobedience?

When has God protected the ministry in the midst of a crisis?

Do we praise Him or only ask Him for needs of the ministry?

Other thoughts:

Now APPLY.

65. God Provides

Our budget right now is the largest it has ever been. The majority is wages for our staff. They work hard and humbly. So having a financially nervous tummy, I am repeatedly learning I must trust our good God. I can't muscle, plan, solicit, or earn all the monetary needs of the organization.

In my frequent prayers for the finances of the ministry, God has said to me "Do you trust Me?" I reply, I do. Again He has said to me "Do you trust Me?" Then I answered "I know You can so please do. I do trust You."

Once I let go, I relax. I can't count how many times I have been to God on this. He is always faithful. He has brought provision from such varied sources it is mind-boggling. We received a check from a woman as a 'thank you' for sending to her mail she dropped in a parking lot at the bank. We received a donation from someone who was given a check at a birthday party to give to the nonprofit of their choice. A bag of quarters was dropped off with no note. A church raised money through bake sales to purchase Bibles so we can give them to clients who need one or need a new one they can understand. We give an honorarium to speakers who provide advanced training. One speaker gave it back!

Have I learned the lesson that God has, does, and will provide? I am still in class. I can say that I trust God with it all. Do I look down at the waters of life and go under from time to time? For sure. Yet Jesus pulls me up, wipes my face and assures me He has it all in hand. We all fail ourselves. God does not fail—ever.

PONDER: Am I trusting in myself or in God?

What gives me a nervous stomach and causes me to lose sleep?

What do I need to do when fear creeps in?

When have I failed myself? How?

Other thoughts:

Now APPLY.

66. *Grace or Consequences*

We all should give grace to each other. No one and nothing is perfect. We are called to forgive one another and move ahead. Yet there are consequences to our actions. Grace is often a replacement word for forgiveness. True understanding of what forgiveness is and is not is very important.

Here is a compilation of one line explanations about Forgiveness prepared by the Eve Center. Contact the ministry for permission to use.

Forgiveness Is Not:

Forgiveness is not overlooking, excusing, whitewashing nor explaining away.

Forgiveness is not you taking the blame.

Forgiveness is not a setup for additional hurt. Remember Jesus tells us His desire for us is to be "as harmless as doves, but as wise as serpents."

Forgiveness is not just "feeling like it."

Forgiveness is not manipulating another into repentance so you can forgive.

Forgiveness is not necessarily a combination of "forgive and forget" if that were so; Christ's blood wouldn't have had to be shed for the remission of our sins. The human brain does not forget. If it has been experienced, it can be remembered for all time.

Forgiveness is not synonymous with trust.

Forgiveness is not minimizing the offense of how bad it really was.

Forgiveness does not mean I never confront or "rebuke" the harmful event/person.

Forgiveness does not open the door for a disrespectful relationship.

Forgiveness does not annihilate healthy boundaries.

Forgiveness Is:

Forgiveness involves walking in grace toward another.

Forgiveness is making a move to change the emotion of unforgiveness within me.

Forgiveness is releasing my right to retaliate.

Forgiveness is a gift you give someone and there is no way they can earn it.

Forgiveness is agreeing with God that someone else (Jesus) has paid for their wrong actions.

Forgiveness is accepting His forgiveness toward them-walking in it.

Forgiveness is trusting Jesus to make it right for me.

Forgiveness is taking hold of personal recovery from the infraction; not just waiting for the other to make amends, that's allowing him/her to be in control of the pain in your heart/life.

Forgiveness is performing spiritual surgery within my soul.

Forgiveness is removing myself as jury, judge, warden, and jailer regarding the offense of the other.

Forgiveness is to quit replaying the event.

Forgiveness is to 'quit counting' the offense.

Forgiveness is to stop looking for replacement, repayment, restoration by/from them.

Forgiveness is going on with TODAY.

Forgiveness is a choice.

Forgiveness is hard work.

Forgiveness is a state of peace, peace within, and peace as a space between you and me. This will look different depending on the infraction; we are called to "walk in peace with all men/women as much as possible."

As a leader it is vital to understand forgiveness as you navigate personalities, individual and corporate. It is a little understood word abused by many manipulators. Corruption of what God says, what Jesus did and the resulting power of the Holy Spirit in grace and forgiveness is foundational to biblical faith. Many are called by God to serve in ministry, mine and yours. Be prepared as instructor to educate and model forgiveness.

PONDER: Do I truly understand what forgiveness is and how it works in ministry?

Does the ministry model maturity and grace?

Other thoughts that kicked up considering this topic:

Now APPLY.

67. Great Idea, Put It In Writing

Often someone comes to me and says "I have a great idea" or "Have you thought about..." Catching me in the middle of a training, speaking engagement, etc. and desiring an involved conversation or a decision right then is not helpful. In order to make sure they feel heard, and to give me time to listen more fully, I offer options.

1. I suggest they put it in writing.
2. Then I can give it proper consideration.
3. Three goals are met by this process:
   a. if the person is serious, they will take the time to write it in an email to me.
   b. it places the ownership of the idea with the person who thought of it.
   c. It removes the idea from me.

If it was *just an idea*, it will go away. I don't waste valuable time for naught. If it has validity, it will fit into proper planning with prayer and many hands involved.

There are times when the great idea is to stay with the person to whom it was given. It is their vision from God to take forward. As a leader I offer next steps of empowerment and reality. Although many great ideas are found while we look at the clouds, the real question is will it be feasible on the hot concrete of life.

PONDER: Do I spend a lot of time on the latest idea?

Is the ministry stretched thin being by everything for everyone?

What is our process for ministry development?

Other thought:

Now APPLY.

68. Grieve

As the organization has grown, I have had to adjust. It started with me doing everything. I loved seeing clients, knowing every volunteer well, touching on all aspects of the work. But there came a time when I couldn't do that anymore. I must constantly remember the purpose for which we are all here, the vision of the ministry. By doing that I can let go of my needs and do what is best for growth. This comes with a cost. I miss being hands-on. I miss the closeness and camaraderie we had in the early years. I grieve how it once was.

A misstep in leadership is not allowing growth because of what I want to hang onto.

Hanging on is not healthy for the organization. Yet there have been many times, by letting others take their place with their way of doing things, I have experienced a sense of loss.

Recreating my role has been a challenge. I like each part I have played.

I have lost my footing several times—frozen by *what is my role now?* There have been months when I continued *to do* yet floundered in *what is my value*. Grief does that. As a leader, and hopefully a good leader, my position has continued to be refined and redefined. It is bittersweet. Letting go is not easy.

With growth, comes new friendships and new levels of relating with staff and volunteers. Maturity in leadership has meant working myself out of a job over and over. As a seasoned leader, I can now impart lessons learned to others in leadership. That is cause for celebration, a fullness in life worthy of the change.

PONDER: Where would I place myself in terms of leadership: new, intermediate or seasoned?

How have I handled change: embraced or been threatened by it?

Have I ever felt frozen, lost in seasons of change in the ministry?

How can I prepare for the next leadership change?

Other thoughts:

Now APPLY.

69. *Guard Hearts, Not Idols*

A leader must identify chinks in one's armor that can let an idol in. An idol is anything that has more importance in one's life than God. Fame, compensation, recognition, credibility, financial stability – any of these can get through to my heart if I am not on guard. It is vital to check my heart to make sure I don't fake myself out.

For example: I must not say that my sole focus on funding is all for the cause. Funding is important, but if seeking a dollar consumes my thoughts and actions, I am out of order. It has become the idol. This can derail a ministry. Instead of seeing what God desires to happen, a slight misstep can lead to decline, one degree at a time. It brings a feeling of being threatened by other organizations' successes. It can make me a hunter and manipulator for money. Trust shifts from God to self.

Another idol is to be a better leader than anyone else. This is rooted in needing approval. We all need affirmation. Knowing and focusing on who I am in God's eyes, knowing the incredible, vast love of the Lord, grounds me in my true identity.

If I need confirmation from man, it is an insatiable pit.

Collecting plaques and awards, having my name noted in testimonies about the ministry, making sure it is known when I am *in the house* at a meeting or event, taints the ministry. Instead of being about what God is doing, it is about me. This can bring resentment from other leaders in my organization and can stifle good growth of new leaders.

Growing closer to God is an active, daily behavior choice:

1. Growing – increasing the percentage of who I am that is focused on Jesus Christ.
2. Closer – not a distant relative but a nuclear relationship.
3. God – if I don't understand who God is, His character, His promises, I don't know Him.
4. Active – not once in a while, not one and done, moving and doing.
5. Daily – can't put this off, there is only today.
6. Behavior – by focusing on God, my sights, my senses, my thinking, my action, my character will be in line with God's will for my life.
7. Choice – using my free will given to me by God to want to be with Him.

Everything and everyone jockeys for my attention as a leader. Nothing and no one should have access to my heart like God does.

PONDER: What have I allowed to impact me beside God?

Ask God who knows you better than you know yourself what your idols are. Then praise Him and ask Him to cut them away so you are not hindered in any way.

What does the ministry have as an idol?

What steps must be made to correct this?

Other ideas:

Now APPLY.

70. HALT, My Version

HALT has been around recovery counseling for years. It stands for "Hungry, Angry, Lonely, Tired." Each word has its obvious meaning. Here is how it applies to leadership.

Hungry: Be careful when you are hungry for the next phase, the next program, or the next big something. When I am hungry, it is as if I need a fix, something to excite me because the day-to-day is mundane at the moment. I or the Board could easily agree to take on another program but that would put the balance of resources at risk. Everything is weakened if we strain toward a new undertaking that is not a good choice or good timing. To combat hunger, feed on the Word of God.

Angry: As a leader I have been frustrated with staff, volunteers, or the board. I must guard my tongue and walk it off. I must find a way to express what I am feeling, decide what to do, and what I need without damaging anyone or the ministry. I can have righteous anger at the societal ills that cause my flock to be wounded. To regain an attitude of joy, praise the Lord.

Lonely: Being a leader is often lonely. You might question this with so many clients, volunteers, and staff around. Yet, I am the one who carries the origin of the vision from God. I alone must be laser-focused on listening and then ensuring we all walk out the mission. It is not a gang of girls just chatting about whoever, whenever. I must, absolutely must, make sure I do not enter into any relationship that may soothe my leadership soul but has a cancerous outcome. Leadership uses every sense and emotion we have—feelings being paramount. Do not connect with someone who emotionally is a bad match.

Binding with another establishes strongholds that are hard to remove from an organization. To be connected, get with other believers in the body of Christ, get in community.

Tired: Well, who isn't?! Attend to yourself. Do not make important decisions when you are worn out. I buy time by saying, "Let me get back to you on that," or "I am tired and this is not the best time for me to decide." Sometimes I would like to just say "Sure" to get the pressure off me, but that is an emotionally based choice, not a thoughtful, prayerful, educated decision. Rest is the best remedy for mental and physical fatigue.

PONDER: Which is my weak spot: Hungry, Angry, Lonely, Tired?

Am I actively in the midst of one of these?

What needs to change?

Other thoughts:

Now APPLY.

71. Head Knowledge Versus Life Knowledge

Beware of the person who comes to your ministry who already knows 'it' all. This person is not open to further teaching. If they are a client, they can repeat all the counsel received through the years from friends, family, pastors, teachers, counselor and doctors. They also have a reason why none of it worked for them. They will make it very difficult for the person who is tasked with offering them services. They have loads of head knowledge but have applied none of it to their life. Offer them a limited, extremely black and white service plan. This makes it easy to determine if they will work the plan or not. They will either quit on their own, or your staff may need to communicate to them that is all we have to offer them. Smile and bid them adieu.

This also applies to staff and volunteers. Everyone must be open to further teaching and growth. Sometimes this 'knowledgeable' person simply needs affirmation of what they may know. But in receiving teaching from your non-profit, this person learns the culture, builds fresh relationships and fits into the team. A staff person or volunteer who always leads with "I" will always be comparing to a past experience and unwittingly distancing themselves from others. How to handle?

Get them on the team.

Do this by inviting them to write down anything NOT in the programs they considered worth adding. Sometimes the person is just trying to mark out their territory, to find their place in the organization. They do not realize they are on your turf.

This acknowledges they have experience to share and affirms you do want their insight. They can then share it through email for directors to review. You are receptive to their input but not to their leading or pointing out a topic that may be left out intentionally that they know nothing about. This places boundaries on their tongue and keeps them on the team but not taking it over. If they are not content with that, then maybe your ministry is not the right match for them at this time. Bid them God's blessings and goodbye.

PONDER: How can the ministry minimize difficult situations?

Do I allow individuals to 'abuse' our ministry?

How do I engage the 'Know It All' in the ministry?

Other thoughts that kicked up considering this topic:

Now APPLY.

72. Honor 'No' From The Holy Spirit

When I am lazer-focused, and have my antennae tuned into a clear Holy Spirit frequency, I know when God says "*No.*" I am purposeful as a leader to make sure I go to our gracious Provider, Protector, and Omniscient Lord BEFORE the ministry goes forward. Even when it looks okay, if I get the '*no*', we pay attention to that. It protects us from getting into something we should not. It is wonderful, even when we don't go according to the easier path He shows, God does work with us. But it is twice as exhausting and much more difficult. God designs the ministry and shows me and the other leaders the *from here to there* steps. When I bow under peer/world pressure and do what everyone else says is good, well…it is not as fulfilling in the long run. There have been times we did not do things the world's way or even the current Christian world's way.

We had outgrown the first office. It was time to move. We prayed and God gave us clear direction about a new location in a nearby church. We approached, met, shared, and waited for a church to pass the proposal through its formal channels. Do note here that we respect process. We waited for three months. Finally, I had to ask straight out if the church was still agreeable or not. We had a time line with which we were working. The pastor said the church could not decide so in a sense it had decided.

Mild panic struck. The team formed a search committee, contacted realtors, and followed the standard familiar route. I, too, was undone because we knew God had provided this next site at that church. We prayed about the next steps, but we took charge. We had not learned about obedience yet. So we followed along the self-soothing, comfortable way of looking for a place but to no avail.

With the deadline approaching for leaving our then current site, I drove around one evening, crying and talking to God. When I gave the search back to Him, really surrendered it back to God, the location was right in front of my car. Really. God plunked down the spot we have today that night. The ministry was not in the church identified earlier. We are in a much better location than we had imagined.

Trust the *no*—it is good for you and your organization.

PONDER: When have I seen God show up in the ministry's time of desperate need?

Have I ever heard 'no' from God? If, so what happened?

When have my team or I chosen the familiar path rather than the unfamiliar way to which God may have pointed?

How can I grow my Holy Spirit listening ear to hear Him more clearly?

Other thoughts:

Now APPLY.

73. *Iced Tea Is Not Working*

I often say "God and ice tea and I am good to go." God is always there, consistent, available and affordable (FREE access) for me. Iced tea for me is just a mild caffeine drip during the day. There are days though when iced tea is not enough. Whether you are a woman or a man, there are chemical shifts in our bodies. Our biology swings. Lack of sleep, what I eat, not enough water, or just a busy week can wear me down. So when two glasses of iced tea don't not energize me, it is time to pause and have my battery recharged another way. It is important to know your personal plug-ins. For me it is to eat lunch alone and read a book. My literary choices are not spiritual, behavioral help books; I enjoy mysteries. It doesn't take long, but I need the pause in each day and sometimes I need a half day off. The forms for recouping must not be medicinal, more caffeine, or unhealthy ways to make your body surge to get the work done. If this is happening, it is bad for your health. Others who are close to you know it, so either they have to cover it up or ignore your behavior. Ignoring takes energy to focus away from you and toward work. But they see your behavior, and this impacts your leadership and obviously the ministry. So know when you need time away, address it proactively, before you are drained. Be human.

By discussing burn down and how hard the job is ahead of time, the team and the Board is aware of the need to recharge and can plan appropriately. No one is caught off guard. There are evaluative points to measure and ensure you remain healthy in your role. The Board must implement vacations and days off, or like many other Leaders/Directors, you will leave the job. Our organization has two paid weeks scheduled into the year; the week of Christmas and the week of the Fourth of July.

Do you want to be remembered for how you leave the job? You were so stressed, so you were let go because you couldn't handle it? Angry, disorganized, burned out? I doubt that is what any leader wants.

Model emotional, relational and spiritual health and when you are ready to exit, leave them wanting more of you!

PONDER: Do I have a plan to assure I remain healthy?

Do I take my vacation?

Do I shut down? Do I leave the telephone, texts, Facebook, email. Twitter, donors, staff, volunteers, and clients at work?

Who on my team needs to take a break?

How will I identify when I need to stop and recharge?

FROM CLOUDS TO CONCRETE

Other thoughts:

Now APPLY.

74. *If Only: Lottery Thinking*

"If only I had $$$ to do…" If only ** company would donate…" "If only I could win the lottery." This magical thinking is not realistic. It is creating a fantasy of the perfect organization. All my cares would be taken care of, millions of people's lives would be improved, the mission would be a reality, I could retire… When this kind of thought occurs, it is a signal I have reached an impasse. I want an easy way out of a hard work day. I want a break. I want… Notice it is all about me even though I *think* it is about the ministry. The odds of winning a lottery are gazillions to one. It is a fantasy.

It is then time to put my feet firmly on the concrete and assess the situation. What do I, as a leader need? What do I as a person need? What needs to get done? Who and what will it take? AND is it realistic?

If you need time alone to draw back, get away from the ministry to focus on the ministry ALONE. Retreat to somewhere you can gaze off at trees or something similar in nature. You will think clearly and pinpoint next steps. If you need time with others, get out of your office-head and be around the clients, the programs. This will engage the other side of your brain.

You will be able to draw a breath realizing that the ministry is doing well.

God is moving, therefore you can now attend to your tasks. Praise God for all that has been accomplished to date. Take note of the blessings. Appreciate yourself and each person who has helped, who is working toward the mission, and pray for those to come.

Don't waste your hard-earned dollars in the lottery. Focus on what God is doing and praise Him for that which He called you to be a part. Dreaming is not doing.

PONDER: Do I fantasize about the ministry and 'if only' scenarios?

Why am I doing this? How can I refocus as the introvert or the extrovert God created me to be?

Other thoughts:

Now APPLY.

75. Incident Management And Reporting

It is one thing to have insurance, it is another thing to have a process for an emergency.

What is your protocol if someone falls in the parking lot? What if someone falls in your offices? What if someone has a complaint? What if you receive a negative message on social media?

It is best practices to have professional resources available for the team. Ask the insurance provider for protocol to adopt. Seek legal counsel when developing the ministry's incident management and reporting. While this is not legal advice, here are important discussions to have:

1. Know what the legal parameters are for your facilities. It could be different if they fall in your parking lot that you own, versus falling in the parking lot that you lease. Regardless, how do you assist? Simply offer them assistance: do they want you to call 911? Are they okay? Recommend that they check with their doctor. Write up an incident report with whom, when, what happened, their response to offers of assistance, and what they say about what happened. If someone else witnessed the incident write down their observations. Give the documentation to your Director. Train your staff on how to be responsive. Document always!

2. If someone is in distress, physically or emotionally, have a step plan to assist. A step plan outlines everything necessary to insure the distressed person is okay. Remember, unless you are professionally trained for these circumstances, it is always best to call the professionals: police or emergency service.

3. Social media prompts many to respond to your organization. For us it has been overwhelmingly encouraging. Yet once in a while we receive a concern in a message. Respect the person who writes. I appreciate the time it takes to bring something to our attention. It is important to have the writer know you heard them. Our steps for this are: acknowledge receipt of communication and invite the person to talk privately by telephone or in person. We want to find common ground and improve our programs where indicated. By seeking to talk, it provides both of you a confidential way to clear up any miscommunication. We are all about privacy and respect. Sorting it out in public is not a proper forum for this. Document all of this as well.

PONDER: Does the ministry have legal counsel?

What are the ministry's emergency procedures?

Does the team understand how to implement?

What is the chain of reporting so I as Leader know what has happened?

Do we document an incident in case of a future complaint about it?

Other thoughts:

Now APPLY.

76. Insurance: General Liability And D&O

It is best practices to have professional resources available for the team. Ask the insurance provider for protocol to adopt. Seek legal counsel when determining the correct insurance for the ministry. While this not legal advice, here are important discussions to have.

"It is expensive." "We don't really need it; we are small." "God will protect us." "We aren't a crisis ministry." "We see only adults, no minors." "No one would sue us, we do a good service for the community." It is easy to explain away anything we don't want to confront. The fact of the matter is a client, volunteer, staff, or visitor could fall on the premises. The coffee maker could be left on all night. An electrical short from the internet router could catch fire. General liability and property insurance may protect those for whom you provide services and the places where you provide the programs. Many venues require proof of insurance before your business can contract to have an event on its premises. Get insurance.

When the ministry began, I knew every person involved well: from every Board member to each working volunteer. I took all the calls for the clients. I was the one who emptied wastebaskets and ran the sweeper. One could believe the false promise that nobody would want to harm me through suing the ministry. Yet

it is often family and friends who bring litigation.

Therefore, it is mandatory that the organization purchase Director & Officer insurance. The role of the Board of Directors ensures that the nonprofit is being run legally. They hold the responsibility. Protect them with insurance. Get it.

PONDER: Do we have general liability and property insurance? Is it current?

Do we have Director & Officer insurance? Is it current?

Does staff have a copy in the staff handbook?

Is there a fully stocked first aid kit on site?

Do we have a working fire extinguisher on site?

Other thoughts:

Now APPLY.

77. Integrity

Integrity is about being the same in public as in private. Over and over, leaders are challenged about inappropriate behavior on the job and outside the workplace. If you are a Board member or a leader who is starting a succession plan, be sure to truly vet any candidate, whether well known to your organization or not. Remember, nothing you do is totally private. As a believer in Jesus Christ, I know He is aware of all I do and all I think. I also know and counsel many to pray that the truth be known and justice served if they are working with a leader who is not acting morally or is behaving unethically. If I am doing my best to walk in truth and honor, then I know I am above reproach. I am human, not perfect. As a leader, I must hold myself to a higher standard. I will stand before my Redeemer God and will reply to Him. I am also watched by all around me, both within the ministry and without.

Transparency is so valuable. I am just me—I am my whole story. It is freeing to be my complete story! As a leader, find your identity and security in God. Then enjoy how you are wired and share how He has grown you to where you are now. Lead as you are made.

Remember your public life and your private life should match – that's integrity.

PONDER: Am I hiding private matters that can impact the ministry if found out?

On a scale of 1-10 (ten being absolute), what rating would you give your understanding of who you are in Christ?

What needs to change about that? What steps will I take to improve the rating?

Am I praying that nothing false be in the ministry that can harm it?

Other thoughts:

Now APPLY.

78. Is This As Far As It Will Go?

There was a time when the ministry grew and reached a good point. Many women were receiving peer counseling. Volunteers were being trained to offer the peer counseling programs. Finances were good. Credibility in the community was good. Satisfaction is what I felt. I wondered if this was the culmination of the vision. I asked God "Is this good enough? I am willing to have this be good enough." In conversation I gave the Eve Center back to God. See, He entrusted the vision to me. He gave me the direction in which to take it. It was successful. So was this good enough and to be continued *as is*? I was not bored. I did not want out. I was not seeking "well done" from God. As a good employee-servant, I was checking with my Boss. I was also ready if there was a next assignment for me that was different going forward. I was content doing the spiritual evaluation of the ministry.

Oh praise my incredible, loving, gracious, good God! He handed it back to me and said "There is more." It was then He gave five subjects that our programs would focus on: abortion, abuse, anger, grief, and relationships. Having specified goals laser focuses growth. It gives security and purpose to all engaging in services. This also opened the door to many more to bring ideas and to learn about these subjects. The end result was more being equipped and more healing taking place. The Board and staff have purposefully moved toward fulfillment of these directives. God sets the vision. Then we as leaders ask. He is faithful to fill in the details for how the mission will grow in depth and breadth. God is not limited. I learned a great deal during this time.

PONDER: When have I given the ministry back to God?

Am I ready if God asks me to move on?

Am I fearful of what next He might next require of me?

Other thoughts that kicked up considering this topic:

Now APPLY.

79. *If You Died Tomorrow, They'd Have To Figure It Out*

When the ministry started, it was just me. Praise God it began to grow right away. It was soon apparent others would be needed in leadership. We had a joke that all aspects of the organization were inside Cinny's head. Everyone had to ask me to know how to do anything. While this was funny, it was vital for the organization's health that I do a *brain dump*. For my own mental health, I needed to unpack what I knew. But how? How was I to let others have the responsibility of leading? How was I to trust they would do as good a job? It was more time consuming to bring others in while at the same time running the show, but I needed to realize that I had to let go and not worry about who and what and how. Keep focused on "What is the point?" It is the Mission and the Vision.

If I trusted those around me, they would grow as they stepped into new roles, just as I did. And if I died tomorrow, God would take care of them and the ministry I started. So I started to help in transition right away. I have continued to provide mentoring thoughts and guidance as asked. No micromanaging—that stifles talent and passion.

I had to get over myself. I was not the one and only one to lead all aspects of the ministry. Holding on too tightly actually suffocates an organization as it grows.

PONDER: Am I holding tightly to the ministry?

Does anyone else have a good concept of the workings of the organization?

If I died tomorrow, would it survive?

What do I need to communicate that I haven't?

What needs to change?

Other thoughts:

Now APPLY.

80. It's Not A Bad Idea, It's The Timing

There is a lot of positive energy at the organization. Each volunteer, as they engage in the basic training, advanced training, peer counseling, and events, generates new thoughts, and new avenues to build and grow further. As a leader every moment is committed to furthering the mission to see the vision fulfilled. Rare is the time I can sit and ponder as I did in the early period of growth.

I want to encourage you leaders.

If the time is not right to implement an idea, capture it.

Get it in writing and put it aside to pray about. Encourage your followers to bring new ideas to you. Be fair and communicate to them that you hear it; but it may not be the right time for it. I had to give up feeling pressured to implement every good idea. I would feel insecure if another ministry was doing something that would also be good at our organization. God may be signaling an expansion of processes or programs for later on. Capture it and then trust God to bring it up again when the time is right.

PONDER: What do I do with good ideas?

Are new ideas coming into the ministry through the staff, Board, volunteers, donors, and for community?

If not what needs to change?

Other thoughts:

Now APPLY.

81. Job Description, Include Prayer

It is rare to see a job description (except at our ministry) that includes prayer time as part of their ministry, with the expectation of spiritual growth for the staff person or leadership volunteer. It is not an item that can easily be quantified, but it certainly impacts the quality of the services provided. If I am not receiving education from my ultimate Boss—God—then how can I grow as a leader? My worldview requires a certain quantity of time to ensure quality of work. I seek instruction, listen for response to my concerns, review my role—limits and scope, receive affirmation and give gratitude for the best boss ever.

This is dedicated prayer time on behalf of the work I do. It is separate from my personal time with God where I bring family, friends, church, nation and world into the conversation with Him. Make sure you and each of your team members have prayer time as part of their priority duties in the job description. Include it in evaluations. Hold it as a standard for everyone who comes through your doors. Here is what the ministry job description includes:

> *Primary functions/responsibilities of _____:*
> *Pray regularly for the ministry*
> *Maintain a healthy and growing relationship with the LORD*
> *Confirm ministry's Statement of Faith*
> *Oversight of programs...*

PONDER: Do I pray for the ministry?

Does the staff pray together for the ministry?

What ways does our culture encourage growing in relationship to God?

Other thoughts:

Now APPLY.

82. Judge Judy, or, Special Cases

Judge Judy' is a TV show I enjoy. Her interrogation style and her clear and at times tough talk in the courtroom is refreshing. Most of all she points out there are always choices. There are better ways of handling struggles. She is ruthless, yet fair. The best lesson she references is to have boundaries. A boundary is where you begin and others stop. It is where you stop and other's roles and responsibilities begin.

There have been two instances early in our history when I broke the ministry boundaries to help clients. It was well intended. We wanted each client to just catch a break. The ministry paid down payments for apartments, two times, two different clients, several years apart. Was this a bad thing? No. Was it the right thing to do? It didn't hurt anyone... or did it? Did we help or enable the clients?

We don't know how those clients are now. We pray they are okay. We don't know if there were other organizations that could have provided the funds. While a donor gave the funds after the fact because they cared, those funds might have gone to the specific purpose of the ministry. Did we play favorites? What if other clients had the same need? We were not being consistent. And time was spent attending to this special situation instead of what God had called us to do.

Since then, protocol has been put in place: we have a list of what we do not do posted on the website. Volunteers and staff are trained about the specificity of the ministry and have lists for referrals for other assistance. By writing out guidelines, we demonstrate caring while staying true to our purpose.

PONDER: What does the ministry do about *'special cases'*?

Have I under the guise of being the leader, broken through corporate boundaries?

Have I put the ministry at risk in any way by breaking the rules?

Is there a team member who seems to always have an exception that needs approval?

Do any protocols need to be changed or enforced?

Other thoughts:

Now APPLY.

83. *Keep It Simple*

It is so easy for me to make a simple thing complicated. It would be wonderful if we could do this and this and this… If we could have a dedicated volunteer or paid staff take care of it, great! But the reality is, as a leader, I must keep what we do simple and clear. Our staff already has much to do. The larger the family of staff, volunteers, and clients, the more important it is to keep communication simple. It is vital to keep the goals and action steps attainable. Can one understand the expected outcome and how to get from here to there? Are the necessary tools made available? Planning is vital to break down a large strategy into manageable bites. This will prevent overwhelming, while demonstrating concise thinking and achievable outcomes. It keeps everyone focused.

Take fund-raisers for example. When, who, and what will be at the event? What is the budget in terms of expenses and what is desired income? How many volunteers are needed? Will food be provided? What is this ministry not good at doing? Reduce pressure by keeping things simple. For instance: we often contract for the meal to be served in order to focus on the program portion with our volunteers. This is costly. Again, what is to gain if the committee is out soliciting food rather than gathering guests to attend? Focus on what you and your ministry do well.

PONDER: How do I over complicate things?

Are we doing everything in excellence for the mission?

Where has communication broken down? What was the result?

Now APPLY.

84. Keep Your Eyes Upon Jesus— Murray Hastings

If you are having a bad day, look up to the Lord. If you are having a good day, give praise to God. In all things, sickness and health, success and struggle, keep your eyes on Jesus. He did it all for you and for me. He gave His all—His life—for you and me.

Murray Hastings was my father. He embodied integrity. He loved to ski and play the guitar in worship at church. He liked several olives in his gin martini. He would rise early in the morning (5ish) to read the Bible and pray for his family and others. He was a minister for fifty years. He was a good church-going man but ran dry serving God in the 1960s. Then he asked Jesus to be his Lord and Savior and he quit trying to be the best at everything in his own strength. Always and in all ways after that, he kept his eyes on Jesus.

When he was dying, he told all of us, visitor, nurse, everyone where to put one's focus: on Jesus. As a leader of a Christian nonprofit, I desire, yearn to, and am sustained by a focus on Jesus. I place time and attention in my relationship with God the Father, God the Son, and God the Holy Spirit. There is *always* more to do. It is easy to be anxious and attend to the needs of the day and plan to get back to God. Stop! Prioritize Jesus. It makes all the difference.

PONDER: Who do I know like Murray Hastings?

What about them do I need to imitate?

Now APPLY.

86. Know Your Kryptonite

What sets you off? Who is a threat? While these are great questions, change the focus. What do I know about myself that could be a threat to the ministry? If you are not aware of any risk you may pose, ask God. He knows you better than you know yourself. After all, He formed you in your mother's womb (Psalm 139:13-16). "God tell me my parts that are weak and need Your strengthening." "God prepare me for when a sharp time in life will cut me in my soft spot." This may feel very threatening, "Hey, I am barely holding it together as it is and now you want me to seek imperfections?!" God, in His infinite goodness and with care, gave me knowledge of two areas in me to be aware of. When I sense these areas rising, I have friends in place and ways to

Protect myself and the ministry.

God has not lifted these human struggles but I stay closer to Him to ensure I am unhurt. By addressing these points about myself, I am stronger, not weaker because I am not caught off guard. I am proactive in turning away from the temptation to think or do something that could harm the ministry and me. Don't be foolish and think you are beyond temptation or distraction. That is *'idol'* talk. Don't think because you work in a Christian nonprofit there is a bubble of immunity.

As you grow as a leader, realize you have an enemy focused on your destruction. It is vital you are aware. One of my weak points was that I wanted to be known, not necessarily for fame but so I would be that someone others would look up to. I wanted to be special, a bit of a local celebrity. This was a danger zone because it would make me feel better than others. Really it meant I was insecure and in need of validation. When a person needs validation, it can be a bottomless tank that needs constant refilling. That filling, that security, can only be filled with the soothing love of Jesus.

PONDER: What do I know about myself that is a soft spot?

Have I asked God to show me any weaknesses?

What do I have in place to turn me from feeble attempts to handle this on my own?

What is weak about the ministry?

What needs to change?

Other thoughts:

Now APPLY.

86. Laugh

It is so easy to be serious, all the time. Yes, funds need to be raised. Yes, rewrites of policies and procedures are needed, agenda items need to be sent to the Board president and statistics need to be gathered to reflect progress on a number of programs.

Laughter is good medicine. Take time to go to the store and read greeting cards, then laugh. Read something that has no mental nutritional value and laugh. Put on a comedy and laugh. The purpose is to allow your brain and emotions to detach from the toxicity of your world. Plan a night out to listen to friends and laugh at their stories.

Refresh your soul in community of others.

Try a new thing: go to a new park for a walk; go to a museum and look at old Egyptian sculpture and laugh at the way it looks like what you might make out of clay. Several things happen when we laugh with others and at ourselves. It shows there is joy to be had. You are a fun person—not all boxed in by work. Best of all, you have fresh stories to rewind in your memory of good times and good laughs. At work meetings, after opening prayer. Share a joke-of-the-day or something funny that happened in the office. Invite others to take turns bringing an uplifting moment at the next meeting. Have staff share successes. So often we focus only on concerns.

PONDER: Do I take myself too seriously?

Am I as fun to be around as I was a few years ago?

When was the last time I relaxed and laughed hard?

Other thoughts:

Now APPLY.

87. Leaders Are Human

Say what? Yes, you and I are human. The difficulty is with responsibility comes expectation. Expectations can hoist you onto a pedestal that is not a good foundation. Any time someone says "Oh, you are Cinny Roy, I've heard about you," I reply that I am just me and I hope it was a good thing they heard! The point is to stay on level ground, firm on the concrete, not elevated in any way. We are peers, with one another. I praise God for the ways He designed me with talents that are unique to me. I also praise God that every person has been as uniquely crafted by our Creator God. I am no better than or lesser than anyone else. I am proud of what I do. But that does not place me above others. If I am off in the clouds, elevated higher than others, visibility is poor. Stay human—you are easier to relate to, and it is not so far a fall as it is from a pedestal.

PONDER: Do I think more of myself than is appropriate?

Do I think poorly of myself? Why?

Other thoughts:

Now APPLY.

88. Legacy: Close The Doors When It's Time

Remember there is a season for everything. The lifetime of some ministries is short. If I am an obedient daughter of our Risen Lord, I am in tune with God's timing. We hope that the successful programs of the ministry will continue and grow, modified to meet the needs of the community. Yet, if it becomes time to say goodbye, that is okay as well. Get comfortable with the thought that your time will end at the organization.

Get comfortable with the thought that during your tenure, you may be required to ask the question "Is it time to close the doors?"

Holding on too long is not good for the memory of the ministry.

Maybe what has been is just that: a has-been. Don't become residue, or a leftover. Have a daily attitude of offering the organization back to God, trusting His will, and His timing. His provision assures you will know when enough is enough. Obedience is success. Then celebrate, with all you have, what has been accomplished. Bless all who have been a part, both small and large. Mourn when it is time to end, then be joyful for what God will call you to do next.

PONDER: Do I hold tight and desire strongly to make sure the ministry last, forever?

Will I be able to handle it if the ministry should complete its lifetime in my tenure?

What does "legacy" mean to me?

Other ideas:

Now APPLY.

89. Lesser Strengths

Visionary, big-picture person—that's me. God has blessed me with the discernment for what needs to be done and how to put meat on the organizational skeleton. Filling in the details, the arteries, the ligaments, is not my strength. Over the years, though, I have had to press into my lesser strengths. I found I am quite capable of writing procedures, addressing processes for work flow, and developing the volunteer handbooks and the staff handbooks. Do I want to do these things? Absolutely not. I am wired to move onto the next thing, the expansion of the vision. Yet in order for the organization to be healthy, it requires my time as a leader to be involved in the details. The lesson I learned, though, was this: when I was working on tasks that were not using my strengths, it wore me out twice as fast. My battery would go low quickly.

Yes, I could delegate. But as the organization grew, I had to be the one to formulate the components that others could then step into. In order for a volunteer or staff person to adopt a role, it needed to be defined. In order for others to provide a service, training needed to be done. In order for the bookkeeping of the finances to be done, the data must be retained. Many will follow, but they need to have someone who will lead.

A true leader can fluctuate to be a macro or a micromanager as needed.

Seek others who possess the desire and skill to complete the tasks. They will benefit if you define it and give it to them to complete.

PONDER: What are my 'lesser strengths'?

How am I doing as a delegator?

Can I identify priorities and complete details necessary for another to assume responsibility?

Other ideas:

Now APPLY.

90. *Letting Go Of Volunteers*

"When school lets out, I am going to stay home." Okay, I thought. "When will you be back, after school begins?" "No" was their reply. I was shocked. She had been a wonderful volunteer coming every week and giving half a day for several years. I felt as if I was being abandoned.

It is very hard not to take it personally when the season for a volunteer or staff member ends. When possible have an exit interview either by you or by another who knows the person who is moving on. What ways would they like to stay connected? Is there anything as a leader you should know, good and bad? The intent here is to garner wisdom from an observant participant.

Do check yourself: was there anything you did or didn't do that might have impacted the decision? But do not overthink it or be riddled with guilt. That won't do you, the ministry or the other person any good.

Send a thank you. Appreciate all that was given. Thank God for this person and pray continued blessings for them.

Then let go.

PONDER: What is our practice when someone leaves the ministry?

What do I think when someone moves on?

Other thoughts:

Now APPLY.

91. *Life And Death Language*

"I could just die." "I could shoot him." "She is such a loser." "Get a life." Our world is starving for love and affirmation. Yet it is full of death language. It is so easy to slide into the current culture of shaming, bullying, and blaming. This is slowly killing someone with words that destroy the inside of a person.

As a leader I hold my tongue.

It is important that we pour into and not drain out of our communities.

Be glad to see someone even if you are busy. Stand up when anyone comes in the door. Greet them warmly. When making introductions, share a way the person has improved your life or the ministry: "I want to introduce Rayanne Wackychick to you. She is a great volunteer here at ---." "This is Roger Knowsmuchtech and he assists us with our technology which is so wonderful."

As believers and followers in Jesus Christ who gave His life so that we may live, how can we talk so much about dark topics? Lift each other up with stories of what God is doing in your life, the life of your team, the lives of the clients, the generosity of donors, the office, and more! Providing a healthy, encouraging environment attracts others to you and the ministry.

PONDER: How do I talk, life or death?

How can I model affirmation and blessings at work?

What needs to change in the ministry's culture about this?

Other ideas:

Now APPLY.

92. *Location, Location, Location*

There are several parts to this section:

1. Right out of the gate

September 1st of 2003 is the founding day of the ministry. The church I was attending, and where my father was the pastor, gave me two unused rooms on the second floor. One was the former school library with old metal shelving and sliding door cabinets. It was perfect for office and meeting space. The second room was the former school's principal's office. It was just right for counseling and to set up a leadership station. I went on my merry way to begin planning for the first training of volunteers in January.

Unbeknownst to me, a colleague in the pro-life arena was on vacation in Canada. She was praying for her father and other loved ones when she said my name popped into her head. While we know each other, it is rare for our paths to cross and word had not radiated out about the ministry yet. When we met later she told me on that she thought it was weird. So she returned to her prayers. Again, my name popped up. She figured she better check in with me when she returned to town.

Jackie called me and asked to meet in October 2003. I headed across town to Pregnancy Center West, Inc. where she was the Executive Director. She asked me about the Eve Center. I enthusiastically explained. Then she handed me a key. She said she was told by God to give Eve Center a west location in storefront space that was open on the first floor of their building! So within two months Eve Center had two rent free, utility-free locations. Lesson? Do not ever doubt God has established His plans beyond any way you could ever imagine designing yourself. Before the ministry was even open, we had resources beyond our needs.

2. Moving day becomes moving year

In February 2011, the organization had outgrown its space at the church. Graciously we had been given several more rooms but we still needed more space. Meanwhile our host church also needed the space. The Board prayerfully reached the decision that it was time to seek another location. My first thought was to form a search committee and find realtors to go about it the way everyone else does. Then we stopped and prayed. With Godly direction we drafted the criteria still used today for seeking new sites. This has kept us focused and served as a tool for communication with potential sites to explain why they had not been selected. This helped to avoid any politics as to why an Eve Center connection's church or building was not chosen.

Our God is so good. Quickly a location was suggested. When God guides, it is as if you open your hand and a feather drifts down into it. The Bible says His yoke is easy and burden is light. Yes, that happens at times. We contacted the church, presented a packet of information, met with their leadership, answered questions, toured the space, approved the space, and waited. And waited, and waited…I kept in touch with the Rector. She assured me that decisions were slow, and she remained encouraging. We waited. After three months we determined we could not wait any longer. We never did get a clear decision from that church. Then the questions began. Did we not hear correctly from God? What went wrong? Why when we were so sure did this location fall through? There was no answer. We knew we had been obedient in following God's direction.

Our responsibility is to obey, leaving the results to Him.

We are successful in our obedience. Now, rather than waiting on the Lord, we rushed to control the situation and started looking everywhere. We saw office space in basements. We saw small and large options. We drove all around. Our budget was small. We could not afford much and our host church needed the space we were currently occupying.

We were tired and feeling defeated. It was now November, and I was feeling the pressure.

One evening I was too early to go to exercise class located near the church where the organization resided. I drove around the area crying. I said 'God, I don't know what to do! We need a new home.' I gave it up to God. Driving along, I saw a low gray building. As I neared it, oh well – it was the fire department's offices. But just beyond was a parking lot and another row of one-level storefronts. I pulled into the parking and got out. There was no signage on the doors, no street numbers, no lights. Mind you it is dark in November, and I was not sure exactly how safe it was for me wandering around. I went to exercise but a mustard seed was now in my hand where the feather had been.

The next morning, I was right back there walking around. I went to the fire department to see if they knew who owned the building. No such luck. So I walked farther down the block of connected storefronts and found a corner door with a paper notice of a business with a phone number. I sat in my car and called. Out of my mouth came the following "Hi I am Cinny Roy, I run a ministry, and we need a new office space. We don't have a lot of money but I would like to know more about this building." Within days we met with Mark and Melisa Lindsay of Quantum Investments. We toured the leaking, dirty, rusty, decrepit space. How does one explain such a God thing? Soon, we signed a lease and the Lindsay's got to work on preparing the offices for the ministry to move in June 1, 2012. They tailored the two storefronts to the design of what we needed: counseling rooms, recovery room, training room, office. It met all the God given criteria that was drafted in February. We learned to

Give it ALL to God. Trust Him, not the circumstances.

3. Growth and expansion

Having two locations up and operational within a year of each other worked. But I do not recommend it without more planning than I put into it. Going from one to multiple locations thins the manpower and stretches the funds. Expanding so quickly weakens the relational needs of early development. The headquarters location absorbed the majority of my time. Therefore, while the leaders of the team at Eve Center – West were amazing (Joanne & Rita), we were just barely understanding the programmatic side of our services and no attention was going into mentoring, training leaders, and building the West team. Lesson: write out the phases of development of your strategic plan. This assists in slowing those who are all "LET'S GO!" and provides a secure way for the non-risk takers to see it is okay to move forward, that change is good and growth is orderly and messy at the same time. It contains the emotion so as not to burn out the leaders, the investors, or the volunteers. It enhances communication and focuses on the mission of the ministry during expansion. This is labor-intensive as it takes time to listen, pray, plan, review and activate. As we have grown, the ministry is stronger for the time we have taken the last five years to slow down and do this or we would not have managed growth.

PONDER: In reading this story, what did I learn?

What preparation do I need to make as the ministry grows?

What am I hearing from God that I must share with other leaders and the Board about how the ministry approaches change?

Other thoughts:

Now APPLY.

93. *Loneliness*

Friends don't always understand it. Family doesn't get it. Sometimes I don't get it, but there is no denying it either. The *it* is the call on your life to do what you do. It is so exciting, challenging, rewarding, and lonely. How can it be lonely when I am around so many people? Friends ask but then glaze over if I share more than a nominal response. It seems no one wanted to listen to me. There have been fun gatherings that I have had to decline due to commitments for the ministry. This results in my no longer being as connected with friends as before. This results in diminished support for me.

It is a fine balance of being fully present for both family and ministry. It is imperative to make sure your spouse and children do not resent the call of God for you. Family wants *me*, not the ministry, when we are together. The needs of family are a priority—as they should be.

It takes godly strength to endure as a leader.

Then there is the boundary of being a leader. At all times I strive to be authentic without being so messy that the office of director loses respect. As a leader, I am human, but I am the leader. There are times to gather with staff and others in the leadership of the ministry. But, that focus is about growing as a team, sharing struggles IN THE MINISTRY—things that pull at us as we grow as Christ followers. Prayer needs for personal cares are vital. We must raise up our concerns that are burdens and tug at our hearts. But it is not a place for close in counseling issues. Do not expect to be best buddies with your co-workers. They are work friends, not social friends. They are friends and co-laborers for Christ. When we overlap friendships and work relationships too much, and changes at the ministry happen where you disagree, the loss can be profound. A friendship as well as a coworker may be lost. We work closely, sharing much, but the ministry mission must remain the priority.

Be wary of expecting them to be that which is not in the job description—to hang with you. Recognize that leadership is at the top peak, a pointed windy spot at the top.

Seek wise counsel that can handle your download of good, bad, and ugly—where you can be heard, supported, confronted.

And know—sink it in deep—that you are *never alone*. You are part of the most amazing four-pack: God the Father, God the Son, and God the Holy Spirit are with you! The Triune God sought you out for relationship and participation in His plan of ministry. Go spend time with God. Tell Him, write to Him, read about Him, and listen to Him. Your soul will feel befriended, heard and loved.

PONDER: What losses have I had as a leader?

Which has hurt the most?

Can I reclaim what was lost?

Do I ask Staff for too deep a relationship?

How do my family or close friends view my ministry work?

Has it drawn me closer to God?

Other thoughts:

Now APPLY.

94. Manipulator: Are You One?

It is very easy to be outgoing in a worldly way. As the founder I have the great honor of meeting with friends and new acquaintances to communicate to them about the wonderful work going on at the ministry. In a sense, I am in sales, inviting others to invest in my nonprofit company. If the intent of the meeting is to present and invite investment, how far does one go? Do I trust God will bring all we need at the time it is needed, or do I turn to my human ways to close the deal? Again, where is my trust? In God or in fallible me? I have learned people do give because of who is involved. They commit to a successful program rather than to fear. But do I point to me or to God as the

One who gave the vision, started the ministry, and leads those who come to serve and come for care?

While I love a *'yes'* when I ask for assistance, I prefer an honest *'no'* if the person will be unable to fulfill the obligation.

Do I try to manipulate a yes, pressuring others into my mold for them? Listen carefully to responses. Assist them in thinking through serving with you. Are the delighted but in the clouds or clear and firmly on the concrete? It won't do you any good if they are foggy. There is nothing worse than giving someone the authority to complete a task only to find out it was not done. A weak *'yes'* is worse than a firm *no*. If it truly will be a struggle, it might be better to wait for a different time to expect assistance from this person in this way. Having realistic expectations prevents resentment on both sides.

Relax and give honor to God and those who work very hard in the organization. Those you speak with will know you are a part of the team but not a team of ONE. This brings a greater investment of their time, talent and resources.

PONDER: Do I in any way manipulate meetings with staff, volunteers, donors or others?

What have I observed in others that is immoral behavior while being masked in Christianity?

PONDER: Do I as a leader truly listen to the replies I receive?

How do I reply when I am told *'no'*?

Is *'no'* an answer the team is allowed to give me?

What do I need to change?

Other thoughts:

Now APPLY.

95. *Message Versus Delivery*

If I took to heart the tone and the words of what people have told me over the years, I would have quit long ago. "You aren't going to do that are you?" "That isn't the best idea." "I don't think you have thought this through." "I didn't think you meant me." My life is like a car. I have accumulated many 'dinks' in my paint from wayward grocery cart comments that fly across the parking lot of life full of offensive comments. Praise God for an everlasting new paint job. Instead, I listen to what the person means to say, and what the message is I am to gain. I then reframe what is said back to the speaker to insure I have understood what was said: "Let's go over how this decision was reached. Maybe I did not communicate clearly, I value your thoughts."

This is enough to subdue the offensive tone. If it is an awkward time, remember you may take the necessary time to consider a correct response. Reply with "Maybe. I'll give it some thought." Then exit. It is okay to leave them hanging once in a while.

Repeatedly I have had to forgive offenders. Sometimes it is the tone. Sometimes it is a class or cultural turn that is awkward for me. Sometimes it is how a gentleman says things. Most of them were not aware that what was said was just not good for me to hear. I forgive so I am not hampered by holding onto the offense. I forgive so that person will remain valued by others, and in forgiveness, I recall the good of that person and pray blessings for them.

If I don't forgive, I suffer, I lose sleep, I am grumpy, I am distracted and less ministry work is done, I eat poorly, and on it goes. I prefer free and focused.

PONDER: Have I ever been offended by the way things are said to me?

How did I handle it?

Have I ever thought about forgiving the person? Praying blessings for them?

Other thoughts:

Now APPLY.

96. *Money Control, Whose Is It?*

It is very easy as a leader to believe the funds raised are mine to control. This is not true. Funds may be given because the investors believe in and approve of my leadership. They may give because they too have experienced a loss or need at some time in life and the services this ministry provides is successful. As a leader, I do impact how the funds are used. But at no time are they my funds! It is vital that I do not blur the lines of the finances. Besides being wrong it is illegal. If I am isolated, or feel under-appreciated, I might feel I am owed an extra meal or a payment for a purchase. Don't slip into the temptation. Face it, no one in nonprofit work makes fabulous wages.

God called me into ministry. God gave me His vision. God has provided investors for the organizations. The money is all HIS. Knowledge of that can be a deterrent from mismanagement of funds. Additionally, make sure the Board is keeping good oversight of all the finances, both income and expenses. Transparency of finances is a requirement for best practices. Two signatures may provide a check and balance for accounting. Online bookkeeping should have more than one administrator. The Board does not owe me anything beyond what has been discussed and agreed to regarding wages. In a place of power, I respect the role I am in, the office of Director.

Give God recognition whenever a financial gift is made. I may assist in the fundraising and processing of accounts, but it is God's calling to others to give that brings in the funds.

PONDER: Have I ever felt I deserved more than I make in wages?

Have I ever directed the funds for personal use?

Are funds being managed appropriately?

When has the Board reviewed the finances and the processes for checks and balances in accounting?

What needs to change?

Other thoughts:

Now APPLY.

97. *Money Does Grow On Trees*

Even fruit-bearing trees take effort to grow to maturity: deep root system, regular watering, sun, etc. The same level of effort is necessary for cultivating donors. Fundraising is not easy pickings despite all the internet would have you believe.

Investors want to give to a winning organization, not to stop a failure from happening. Some say "God will provide" and yes, He does, but He enjoins us in the process. We tell the story of what He does and will do. We ask for donors to water the earth of our programs. Then we, the staff and volunteers, prune out, graft in, protect against varmints that could ravage our programs, shade our clients, and invite many to enjoy the fruit of all our labors. There are various stages of growth, and different partners are interested in different parts of our tree. Some like the dirt, some like to see the whole field and how this tree impacts other trees in the community. Some focus on the tools needed to care for the ministry tree. Others like partnering with birds/volunteers or are delighted by the shade of the trees for the clients. Others like to climb to the top of the tree and look out to see other trees, learning from their board members and staff in order to do the best job here. If as a leader I embrace all the help I can get for this tree, then the many who are around it, love it, have experienced it will give from their trees—

investment in lives builds heart engagement that brings financial fruit.

Remember fund raising is as labor intensive as the programs of your non-profit.

PONDER: Do I resent fundraising and what that entails?

Do I procrastinate learning about and advancing the ministry regarding money?

What help do I need from the Board?

Other thoughts:

Now APPLY.

98. No Drinking On The Job

Regardless of whether you enjoy an alcoholic beverage or not, do not drink while on the job. If you are representing your organization, abstain. It is important not to reflect any stumbling point for those who look at you as the face of the nonprofit organization. If you are a guest at any corporate function, even if you are not officially there to represent the ministry, it is best to abstain. If the event is social, such as a wedding, ask yourself if you are there simply as a friend of the family's or is the invitation because of your nonprofit affiliation?

Remember you are being watched. Acknowledge if you enjoy a cold beer or grew up with Kentucky bourbon. It is okay to admit that abut also to say you prefer to enjoy one another day. Be GRACIOUS. If you are served something not to your liking, thank the one who brought it. I have held glasses before only to put them down a few minutes later. Prepare a reply that does not demean the person offering the alcohol: "thank you, but tonight I prefer…"

PONDER: Do I enjoy an alcoholic beverage?

If I do not, what do I think of those who do?

What is my professional stance about drinking at events?

Other thoughts:

Now APPLY.

99. Not Always Right

Over and over I ask for a grace card. This is forgiveness as a token. One sweet volunteer even printed a whole deck of cards with my profile on the cover of the cards so that I could hand them out—I need that many! Why grace cards? Because I mess up and often. It is important to admit before God and man when I forget, don't think of something, offend, blunder, and more. As a leader I am not perfect at all.

What to do when I am not right? First is knowing that I am not always right. Many people truly believe that what they think, say, and do is the right way, the only way, and not negotiable. This type of leader projects perfection (in their mind), forgetting being humble and transparent models reality for others. It is hard because no one wants to show inadequacies. Yet, it is freeing to confess or admit, smile, and ask for grace. I learn and move forward. I can be harder on myself than anyone else. So acknowledging the need for a grace card lifts the pressure, brings a smile, and offers value to another by asking for forgiveness and care.

PONDER: Am I afraid to show I am not perfect?

Whose standards am I trying to live up to? God's or man's?

How do I handle correction?

Do I lie to cover my failures?

Who is safe in my life that I can talk to about my blunders? Who will tell it to me straight while having my back?

Other ideas:

Now APPLY.

100. Not Even The Christian World's Way

Trying to abide by the ways of the world is exhausting. Our organization doesn't even do things the Christian world's way. I have observed ministries that boast of being led by God, but their "talk" doesn't seem to match their "walk."

We were meeting with pastors on staff at a sizable church about having a location in one of their facilities. One pastor asked me about our recruiting process, how did we entice people to our programs. Being a small start-up at the time, our recruiter was, and still is, God. I told him that we do not have a staff person or a budget to recruit. We pray and place our needs before God. As He responds, we then step out to share in joy not under duress. You could have heard crickets in the room. We have and will continue to see God move ahead of us, preparing many to come for training, to come for care, and to come to be a part of the successes. We work with joy, but we do not toil with resentment.

Every ministry does what they do a little differently. This is part of the beauty of diversity in ministry. This is what is glorious about our God. We are free to be about His agenda in ways that reflect His leading and our own talents. Your organization may have a recruiter. You may be wizards at social media. You may telephone individuals. No matter. If it is of God, do it His way.

PONDER: Do I listen to how others operate in their organizations?

When I do, do I feel like I need to do it 'that way'?

What plan can I put in place to solicit engagement?

Is God really the one I trust and ask as I sort out what next in the ministry?

Other thoughts:

Now APPLY.

101. One Decision Maker; A Partnership Doesn't Work

Someone has to have the final say. There is one leader, and you may be that one who is responsible for the decision making. If there are two or more directors, carefully define who is responsible for what decisions so there is no conflict. In our organization, one director has responsibility for marketing and community relations. Therefore, they have the final say for anything that is under their jurisdiction. Value insight from others, but the buck stops with them for that department. They should be ready to support the decision showing thoughtful and prayerful consideration.

If the ministry has joint directors, what happens if they do not agree? It could cause a disruption with both vying for supporters among staff and the Board. Again,

delineating who is the final decision maker for each area of the non-profit will prevent a feud and potential disruption.

You as the Executive Director, the Vision Keeper, are responsible for the final determination of best practice for the organization regardless of authority placed in the hands of a team member. Authorize the team to make decisions. Respect they must learn through experience. Only intercede if harm may come to the ministry.

PONDER: Are roles with decision making authority clearly defined?

Is the authority of each leader upheld and recognized?

Who is undermining your authority?

Other ideas:

Now APPLY.

102. *Organizational Boundaries*

There have been times that various churches and nonprofits have wanted the ministry's services to be a part of their program offerings. That speaks highly of all the amazing work of our staff and volunteers. The God-given direction to our organization is to be separate from but supportive of the Church. Being an independent entity has provided safety for women who are church attenders. Many women have been hurt in church. Some have been abused by church leaders. Some have been pressured to accept teaching they do not believe is Biblically based. Others have not been able to hear good teaching because of their losses and lack of understating of who God is. Some women do not feel safe in church. Some don't want anyone at their church to know their issues. We also see women who do not have biblical faith in their background. These are a few of the reasons we set organizational boundaries.

We do offer what we can to churches and other ministries such as announcements, speakers, training, and print materials. We desire to come alongside the Church, yet we cannot be everywhere for everyone. There are reasons we ask clients to come to the ministry sites. We can ensure confidentiality, safety and consistency in our environment. These are core values to our organization.

Even when a request to assist comes from an influential leader or church many times bigger than we are, the ministry remains dedicated in time and with human resources to the purpose God gave us and the way He has shown us to fulfill the mission. It is not a matter of choosing one over the other. As God directed, we are to stay focused in pursing that directive.

PONDER: How have we been stretched too thinly to provide for other ministries?

What are the boundaries and criteria are established as to who we offer our programs?

When have I or another key leader broken through our boundaries, even for a good reason?

How can I establish criteria to evaluate a situation that challenges the programs we provide?

Other ideas:

Now APPLY.

103. *Passion Versus Love*

I absolutely, completely, always love my amazing husband. He knows me as friend, love, and wife. He is my encourager, sustainer, and stabilizer. We were married in 1980. He knows me as we have had careers, cares, children, aging parents, adventures, and more. We have little sayings that are intimate between us. Many a time I have said, and will do it again right now: I could not do what I do if he was not 1,000% in it with me. Bruce is a *huge* part of who I am today.

Yet I am passionate about the ministry and seeing lives changed for all eternity. Something ignites in me as I talk about the vision that is now a reality. It is what drives me to think, plan, go over, and share. It is foremost in my mind much of the time. It gives me a smile, a boost; it jazzes me. There is always more to do, and that gives me more to think about and be excited to see happen.

Passion swings high and swirls around—that is how as a leader I feel about this thing that was birthed from a call by God to me. Yet just as God called me, He may turn my focus somewhere else someday, and that is okay. The passion for ministry may end. Love is a through and through longing to be with a person: mellow yet consuming, different from passion. Love lasts forever and is a forever commitment.

Make sure those you love understand they matter the most, even if it looks like the passion for your mission is more intense. Passion can fade. Love is complete, deep and long.

PONDER: Do I love, love, love those closest to me?

Do they know I love them or do I act more as if I appreciate them?

Does the ministry come between us? How? What do I do when that happens?

Other thoughts:

Now APPLY.

104. *Passion Versus Skill Set*

Various sources recommend having individuals with specific skill sets on the Board of your organization. I have found that individuals with passion, energy, and love for what the ministry's mission are more important. Have enthusiastic, hands-on folks who will work together and bring in the resources necessary to see the vision and mission to fruition. There is a sense of comfort in filling a position on the Board with someone skilled in a particular ability, but that does not translate automatically into action. If Board members are included out of obligation but are not intentionally engaged, then no support is offered to the Director. This is a main reason why top leadership turns over in nonprofits every few years.

Each of our Board members is active in the ministry. They are excited about the mission. They want to grow personally and to grow the ministry. They are open to learning and being led forward. There are many opportunities for board training through SCORE (www.) or boardwalk.org. Our board provides oversight. They understand the requirement to make sure the organization has a plan for sustainability. They ensure it conforms to the laws for a nonprofit, and is transparent to all who are interested in how their investments are utilized. All can learn how to serve on a board of a nonprofit; not everyone cares enough to put hours into being in leadership this way.

As important, the Board provides a safe place for me to share the excitement of day-to-day operations, where I see the ministry going and its needs. Then with staff, they formulate a strategic plan to get from here to there. We have brought in consultants and others on subcommittees to teach us. I'll take passion any day before skill set. Having both is a win-win, but not every organization has to have only skilled board members.

PONDER: What is the enthusiasm level of your Board?

Has the Board received training on the role they have?

Are they engaged? Have you given them information on what you need for the ministry to grow?

What is your relationship with the Board? Are you boss to report to or a supportive team member?

What needs to change? Does the Board need more members?

Other thoughts:

Now APPLY.

105. *Patterns*

"Once is once, twice is a pattern, three times is a habit." This is a *Cinnyism*. I have coined several sayings over the years. Working with a vast array of people holds a fascination for me. Each has wisdom; each has quirks. I find that repetition is a good indicator of behavior. In the Christian world forgiveness is demeaned by many as a quick way to get past one's own bad moves. In ministry, it has been thrust at me: "Forgive me, I forgot…" or "Forgive me, I know you had asked that…" We are given the command to love one another as Christ first loved us. Yet there are boundaries. I will not hold something against the offender. Yet I will hold to a limit of what is acceptable in attitude and action toward me and the organization, be the person a volunteer, a client or a Board member.

Document when necessary to prevent mushy memories. Stick to facts rather than the emotion of the situation. A best practice is to have expectations laid out in writing beforehand. When a client called and wanted to bring her puppy to her appointment or she would not come—well…we do not have accommodations for either small children or pets. Yes, she needed to come for care, but we would not abandon our structure for her. She decided not to come back. One day she showed up—with the puppy! No appointment. We walked her outside, petted the puppy, said *glad to see you*, and it was over in five minutes. Here was a pattern of pushing against the ministry structure.

A wonderful volunteer was not keeping to the written policy with respect to seeing clients only at our locations, not *off site*, as it is called. She was wonderful, but do we make exceptions that can bring harm to the whole ministry? No. She was reminded, both verbally and in writing that if she continued she would no longer be a volunteer with us. If the volunteer persisted, the client would also be notified, and any future support she would give that former client would be at her own risk. She decided she would rather do her own thing. We put all it in writing, wished her well, and off she went. God gives us the right of free will. We respect that. However,

free will is not a free pass to do your thing at our expense.

PONDER: How do I handle repeat offenders, those on staff or volunteers who continue to cross the line?

Are there any *protected* individuals, those who are permitted to do as they choose because they are donors or community connected?

Have I written procedure for these incidences?

Other thoughts:

Now APPLY.

106. People First Always

Care of the clients who come to the ministry is the entire point of our existence. While paper and processes and protocol are important, nothing and no agenda item is more important than the precious daughters of God, regardless of whether they know they are or not.

Our culture is clamorous: noisy with everyone's opinion, judgment, blaming, and shaming. Our organization provides a safe, confidential place to be heard, to heal, and to grow. Anyone who comes to me will have my time. Yes, as a director, I am busy. What woman (and man) in America is not busy? To know that you can be heard, that your thoughts, feelings, observations, and questions are valued by another, is huge. *You*, the staff, volunteer or client, are of infinite value to me. God's people come first, always; I

encourage leaders to always and in all ways be there for your clients.

Busy? Then set a time limit or schedule a time to talk later. I have used a timer, literally, to keep me on task. If a telephone call or someone stops by. I say *Yes, I have ten minutes*, knowing that either we will sort it out in twenty minutes or schedule more time another day.

Jot that person's name somewhere to pray for them, then send a quick text or email note the next day with an affirming message, maybe with a Bible verse included: "Hi—, good to see you. Just praying that God will support you and be with you today. Fondly or Hugs or blessings…" Be a clear voice of encouragement.

PONDER: What is my attitude about being interrupted?

Am I always behind because of people stopping into the office or contacting me by telephone?

What needs to change to improve this in my leadership?

Other thoughts that kicked up considering this topic:

Now APPLY.

107. *Photos And Testimonies*

"A picture is worth a thousand words", or something like that. Be sure to take photographs at all your events, of workers in the office, clients, volunteers, your building—whatever. *Don't* post the photos without the written permission of the person. We have women who are volunteers who do not want their image on Instagram, Twitter, Facebook, on the website, or in print. One of the forms for our volunteers to consider during training is a written permission to photograph them. Some are okay if it is a group shot, but no individual photo or caption to include names. We respect their reasons, shared, or not. Some do not like how they look in pictures. Others do not trust the internet and fear the misuse of images posted. Others do not want toxic family to have any access to their lives. Lesson:

do not assume—ask. Get written permission for all published photos and testimonies.

Take time to solicit testimonies for the ministry. Written comments are excellent content for newsletters, thank you notes and social media postings. The same rules apply to testimonies as to photos. Secure permission to use. Clarify if the person's name or first initial or anonymous is preferred. If the organization provides programs around sensitive issues, make sure confidentiality is maintained. Edit carefully.

PONDER: Does my ministry have a policy about photographs and testimonies?

Are there individuals who we need to back tack and document permission?

What ways does my organization utilize photos and testimonies:

Now APPLY.

108. *Preparing For Emotional Conversations*

Our culture today avoids face-to-face confrontation, preferring to hide behind in social media and rant. Except for mediation training or self-education, there is no course to practice for how to confront one another. It is fraught with emotion because one or more parties feel wronged. Sigh. It is not easy to criticize another as our society considers criticism a negative. Nor is it easy to have one's own errors to light. So prepare. I have drafted steps for your consideration:

1. Document. What is it that happened or didn't happen? When did it happen—be specific. Why is this an issue?
2. Set resolution as the goal; what are the options for learning and moving forward?
3. Self-assess:
    a. Is there a part of what has occurred that I need to own?
    b. Did I not communicate clearly?
    c. Did I ask for something of someone who could not deliver what I wanted? Did I have unattainable expectations?
4. Write down what the goal is of the face to face: Discussion with altered outcomes established? Reprimand with goals for rectifying the situation?
5. Practice *I* statements not *you did* or *you didn't.* This prevents accusations that lead to defensive posturing and a lose-lose situation.
6. Talk it out with wise counsel to gain another perspective from an objective person. They may caution you to wait or encourage you to proceed to prevent harm to the relationship and the ministry.
7. Pray. Ask God for His timing, for His wisdom, and for His tender yet firm leading.
8. Meet face-to-face; not over the phone or by email. Know when you call and say "We need to meet," they will most likely ask what it is about. We all go into guard mode. Try to see the person as soon as you can, so it does not build emotional walls in both of your minds and time isn't lost.
9. Do not meet over lunch or dinner. Either one or both of you will want to separate after you talk. This is not a fellowshipping-over-bread time.
10. Get right to it. They will sense this is important, and it is best to be crisp.
11. Do not defend yourself but speak using facts, and then listen. Stay on topic. Do not be led off-subject. Stick to "I am concerned by…" "I would like your perspective…" "About___, let's discuss what will (not should) change…" "Thank you, I value your thoughts. I will put this in an email so we capture our thoughts on this." "Anything else I should know? Thank you."
12. Document and enact the action that were discussed. Then breathe. Being a leader is not easy. Take a bit of time to process your emotions, and handling of the conflict. *Do not* go talk about the person with another staff

member. Remember your position is leader. Others will watch and follow your example.

Surprise and anger were my immediate emotions. Three days earlier I had met with the head of a ministry that was, by agreement, using one of our meeting rooms for a recovery group. This person had received in writing the rules regarding the agreement several weeks prior. We met to review and insure all expectations were clearly articulated for both sides. An email reiterating the conversations and the rules had followed.

I received a call that a blatant abuse of the identified, agreed to, boundaries had occurred. Rather than entertain thoughts of destruction of said person, I breathed, asked for clear examples with time of events and who was present. I thanked the caller. I prayed, wrote out the next step which was termination of the agreement and dialed the allegedly offending leader. Although apologies were profuse, this required immediate action. Firmly I stayed on topic which was the agreement would cease effective immediately. The leader let me know the decision was not well received.

After the conversation, email documentation to the various ministry staff was sent. I also called those immediately impacted to listen and affirm.

When conflict arises, the underlying cause is often personal.

I did not model this well early on in the ministry. I tried to soothe everyone, but it became an emotional quagmire, which is dangerous. When I would try to please everyone, it just got messy. I fumbled. I was not leading but appeasing. Praise God, there were not difficult issues at first, and I learned to figure out how to keep my emotional triggers in check. I now lead and try not fumble.

PONDER: How do I handle emotionally charged conversations?

Which conflicted situations have been handled well and which have gone poorly?

What did I learn from this?

What of the above steps can I put in place in the ministry?

Other thoughts:

Now APPLY.

109. Public Speaking

"Would you come tell about your organization?" This can generate excitement or fear for you. My recommendation is to always accept, then find out the details.

1. Date, location and length of time for your presentation.
2. Who is the audience? It is very different to speak to a congregation than to a room of high school students.
3. What is the purpose for your coming? What does the host want to be the outcome? This will impact your preparation.
4. Is this a PSA – Public Service Announcement (brief 2-4 minutes with handout), or, education about the ministry including testimonies of clients?
5. Is there an opportunity to publicize your coming? Do they want information to put in the church bulletin, on their website and Facebook page? Do they have a logo you can attach to announce your presence on your organization's social media? This shows community engagement.
6. How many will be in attendance? Can the host print the handouts or should you bring them?
7. What materials should you have for the audience?
8. If appropriate may your organization set up a table of information for attendees to view before or after the event?

Often the host has not thought of the above considerations. It will make the occasion have a better result.

Prepare. You know the ministry because you are the leader. That does not necessarily indicate you are proficient in telling in direct, clear fashion specifics. It is amazing how nerves can block the brain from bringing forth articulation.

Practice. Leave them wanting more. Be sure to respect the time limit you are given. Write out the main bullets you wish to give, then listen to yourself OUTLOUD, and note changes. Time yourself.

Take someone with you for several reasons:

1. The Disciples went in pairs. Bible says so.
2. This begins training others to be spokespersons for the ministry.
3. Your partner can pray for you as you speak.
4. You can receive honest feedback about the engagement.

PONDER: Does my ministry have a public presence?

How can I draw interest in the organization?

Who can I ask to be a speaker-in-training? What do they need to learn?

Other ideas:

Now APPLY.

110. Put It In Writing: Agenda And Minutes

As a person who thinks out loud, I don't always remember what I said. That can be a problem when I need to attend to what was discussed. How can I expect another to know what we agreed to? It is important to have a recorder—someone who takes notes in meetings. Or if this is a single encounter, capture what was said immediately after the meeting and send it by email.

This documentation is good for both of you. It is a tool for referencing, if there is a discrepancy about what was said and what the steps are moving forward. It is also important to follow up with written summation, as some interpret differently than others. Healthy communication requires back-and-forth engagement between all parties. This is also important historically. As others enter the ministry, they can see how a process or program direction was established that is in use today.

Here is a formula for working in meetings:

1. Insert a header with ministry name, committee or purpose of meeting
2. Make a table in a word document
3. Left column is the agenda item or talking points
4. Right column captures what was decided
5. A third column can be added to put who will attend to the task of what was decided with the reporting date.

Example:

Item	Next Step	Who/When
Year to date expenses at satellite locations	Get $ data from Kathy	Cinny will contact her and send to Sue
	Sue will meet with Managers	Sue will report at next director meeting
		Note: put on 2017 budget list for review

Insure all parties are in receipt of the summation within a week. If execution is expected prior to the next assembly, all must have written expectations in hand well ahead of time.

PONDER: How do our meetings to stay on topic?

Do I capture well the actions to attend to?

What needs to change in our processes about meetings?

Other ideas:

Now APPLY.

111. *Remembrance*

Always celebrate everything that has taken place. Be sure to archive photos, papers, and newsletters. Collect the stories of how the ministry started and who was there, the highs and lows and the growth. Remember to thank all involved as you go along. Remember that love and enthusiasm God placed in you to start it all in the first place. Laugh at the bumbles and smile at the sweet successes.

I receive calls every now and then from lovely folks who would like to ask questions about how the Eve Center operates, how it got started and an account of the struggles. It is wonderful to listen to and encourage them. They too have a heart for ministry. They have a vision and are just starting out. They may be in the trenches and are seeking wise counsel. Share what you have learned with others.

Do not be a Scrooge with your knowledge.

Joyfully answer when asked how you did it. You will be reenergized by recounting how far you have come.

PONDER: Has any one asked me about how I got into ministry?

When they do, am I open, eager, encouraging, attentive, listening, offering, serving?

If not, why?

Other thoughts:

Now APPLY.

112. *Say What You Need*

Take one for the team. The ministry team is everything and so there are times when I must endure a struggle silently in order to benefit the ministry and move forward in growth. But, there are times when the weight can be too much. There are times being a leader is a negative force. I lead. That means one, solo, at the front, the head. And if I do that too much of the time, my perspective gets skewed. Others will assume all is well with me, which leads to more alienation.

I had to learn to break that mold. If I was struggling with how to direct the ministry, or if I needed a break, or needed affirmation or support, I needed to indicate that. Remember

no one can read your mind.

Passive hints don't work well either. If I dropped a hint and it was not picked up, then I would get mad inside and just shut down and be more on my own. That is not a healthy way to operate. Many leaders burn out trying to direct by themselves. Rather than clearly communicating when help is needed, they quit, find another job, retire or get fired because something happens. Who is responsible? The leader is.

Gary Chapman is the author of *The Five Love Languages* (1992, 1995). It defines five areas that the majority of people say shows them love. They are touch, time, service, verbal affirmation, and gifts. It is important to know what yours are. Take the assessment. Make sure others know and pour into your love tank in the ministry and at home, work, school, or church. When we aren't being loved, we are vulnerable to unhealthy ways of getting filled up. Mental gyrations kick up: So-and-so doesn't get me, isn't the friend I thought, is not supporting what I do, doesn't know what I need… This brings a disconnect due to sinful thinking. So reach out to the Board President. Make sure the Board knows to affirm you in a meaningful way.

Humbling as it has been, I have said "I don't know how to…" or "How should I do…" or "I feel like I am not doing a good job." Those who care about me will say, "Of course you are," but sometimes I need more. As a leader, the supporters forget that while I am dishing out affirmation to others, I need some as well. This comes not in the form of awards or public accolades, but from simple words like, "Hey, I see you and know this is a lot. Keep on going. You are super." So make sure you tell others to give *you* a card, a hug, a call, a comment, or lunch while asking you to share whatever you want to. And if you are supporting a leader, make sure they get encouragement from their peers and the Board.

PONDER: Am I silent and always taking the hits for my team? Why?

Do I gratefully accept ways my team 'love' on me?

What do I need to encourage me?

Who can I ask to support me that fits my love language?

How many hits have I taken? If many, this deserves review.

Other thoughts:

Now APPLY.

113. *Scout Versus Wagon Train*

Back in the days of cowboys and covered wagons, a wagon train had scouts. These would go ahead, out of view, over hills and through valleys to scout out the passage for the people to go through. They would return and announce the best direction forward. This is what being a visionary leader is all about. I am off over the hills to anticipate which way we should go next. When I share with the other leaders and the Board the next mountains and the next goals to ascend, I am raring to go *now*. I don't want to wait.

As a leader, I have had to learn that it takes time for those in the wagon train to understand why a particular path was chosen. Giving them this time helps keep the train together. Just for word to travel from the front to the cook wagon at the end of the train takes time. By then it is *old news* to me but a revelation to those farther back. The wagoners trust me as a scout-leader, but they are also discerning, because they are strong folks who have a right to understand why we may go over a mountain rather than through a valley. For their protection and unity in the possible face of attack, taking time to prepare them is vital. So at times I have to get off my high horse and ride in the wagon.

Loyalty comes through relationship. Earn respect as a scout then join your team.

PONDER: Am I taking time away with God to see over the next hill in order to lead the ministry forward?

Am I patient in the process or hesitant about change?

Do I engage others so all understand why we are going forward in a particular way?

Other thoughts:

Now APPLY.

114. Self-image Versus God's Image Of Me

Some leaders think more highly of themselves than is realistic. Some leaders are insecure, doubting their calling and ability. One must be secure to handle the onslaught of questions that come with leadership. In order to be prepared, a continual assessment of weaknesses and skills is beneficial to grow. But, at some time, doing it in one's own strength fails. I must keep my focus 'up', on Jesus. I must understand that God so loves me that He came here to stand in the gap where I fail. He paid ahead for all my missteps. He knows all my faults yet sees me as holy and without fault. Because of what Jesus did, I stand before Him covered in His love. (Ephesians 1:4).

I know by experience that God cares for me. He cares deeply about me, whether I am eating potato chips or praying for the ministry. I have acknowledged I can do nothing right all by myself. I acknowledge I need God in my life and in my work. I can't imagine being a leader without Jesus by my side. At some time, I will fail myself if I am a god unto myself. I am a beloved daughter of our Risen Lord. He has the best in store for me at all times. I trust that and focus on that. When I focus on myself, I fail.

PONDER: What happens when I focus on myself?

What are the circumstances when I am more apt to doubt?

What are the regular lies that run through my mind that are not of God?

What do I do with these?

Other thoughts:

Now APPLY.

115. Sleepless Nights

There is no denying there are sleepless nights as a leader. *What ifs* abound in the dark. One here or one there is normal. It is not possible to avoid them altogether. Yet there are a few signs to be attentive to. If you start to lose sleep every night, pay attention to this. Something is wrong.

Your system is leaking symptoms of trouble by corrupted sleep.

If it becomes three or more nights in a row, your body is altering its sleep pattern, and it will be harder to amend. Assess your options:

1. Lessen caffeine intake (stop after lunch or by midafternoon for sure).
2. Make sure you have exercised, but not within three hours of bedtime.
3. Get a physical if it has been two years or more since your last one. Women struggle with thyroid, and pre- and menopause. All of these can impact one' biology.
4. Consider the use of over-the-counter sleep aids. There are many to choose from. Ask your doctor or the pharmacist.
5. Prayer works for some or can bring more spinning thoughts around the issues. If you do pray, focus on anything other than the issues that keep you awake or woke you up. One way to do this is to worship God.
6. Make a list. Maybe your home has been neglected. Maybe there are errands to complete. Write out everything that may need you to check on so you can check it off in your mind.
7. Talk it out. Seek out your wise counsel. Often we keep concerns in our heads. Concerns need to be given a voice and sorted out. Have you been taking one for the team? Are you frozen into inactivity because of not being sure which way to go? All the *what ifs* need airing. Hope can be found, a plan made and then you can lay down the concern in another room than your bedroom and go to sleep.
8. Take longer time off. You may need a vacation, a change of scene or a different role.

Sometimes God awakens us so we know something is coming. He is alerting His leaders. Praise as He forewarns you. Have an emergency meeting with Him. Note what you receive. Then rest. But if you experience general loss of sleep, then review #1-8.

Take the time to figure it out. You are frail as a leader without sufficient deep, satisfying sleep.

PONDER: How is my sleep?

When was my last physical?

What is keeping me up at night?

What fears need to be taken to Jesus?

Other thoughts:

Now APPLY.

116. *Spiritual Road Crash*

Many of us are old enough in our relationship with the LORD to understand this next leadership lesson. I *do* know to spend time with my Boss. I *do* know to listen wisely and follow His leading. If I remain in Him, He remains in me. I am under His umbrella of protection. But when I dash out into the sun or rain of life, thinking I know what to do, I will fall flat on my face and experience *spiritual road rash*. Scraping along the concrete hurts; it is unsightly, exhausting, and takes a while for the scabs to heal. When I have fallen there have been times when I have taken others down as well. Time and honesty are needed to heal all involved in my spiritual road rash.

Wonderful materials were provided to us by a local author for establishing a new ministry offering. We were thrilled. In my excitement I did not take the time to discern whether or not this material should even be considered for formulation of a new program. We sped up and skipped several necessary vetting steps. This resulted in a weak program without proper leadership training, and expense in time and money. It faltered. It fell flat. We were forced to rethink and start over again. It was a painful time.

Having done that several times in my 'know-it-all' eagerness, I learned my lesson. I am disciplined to pause and hold onto my amazing, wonderful, PROTECTOR so as not to fall. Avoid spiritual road rash—stay with your protector.

PONDER: Have I ever experienced spiritual road rash?

What did I learn? How can I avoid it?

Other thoughts:

Now APPLY.

117. *Success More Than Anything; Wrong God*

"I'll show them." *Proving something* is a dry desert path to take. It is based in being wronged and proving you are right at whatever cost. Desiring to succeed is a good thing. We seek improvement in our world. We yearn to make things right. But do not accomplish this by destroying others along the way. A lie that you may be living as if it is a truth is not the Truth. Jesus is the only Truth that should be your motivation. Camouflage blinds others to your true intent. You may say you are serving God. You may want to equip and grow others to serve in the same way as your organization. But your heart is not hidden from God.

You may run the race of your life to find it was all for nothing because you cheated about where the finish line really was for you.

A hardness, a tough edge, unwillingness to give grace and forgiveness is not sectioned off into just one area. Those walls affect your leadership. Others who are perceptive will see through your mask.

There is no way to deal with this but at the foot of the cross, giving up your agenda for what God has for you. He is all knowing. He is holy and does not care for us to think we can outsmart and use Creator, Redeemer, Healer, for our own puny needs.

I came to realize that I did not need God to show up and do a miracle in order to have value. God did a miracle by paying the ticket in life's movie so I could sit in the front row, recognized and welcomed into His love. I could not change anyone's thoughts about me. I could only accept what God says about me: He LOVES ME!! Even if I was the only person on earth, He would have still come to do what He did for me. He paid the price of my rebellion, my self-value, my self-loathing. He gave me a new start and new guidance. So when I am focused on my God, it is easy. I quit trying to be god. Then I am successful

PONDER: Why am I in ministry?

Whom would I like to show I am better than? (Get real here)

Has this steered the ministry toward goals that are not truly honest but my hidden agenda?

Other thoughts that kicked up considering this topic:

Now APPLY.

118. Success Versus Obedience

What is success to you? Is it a plump payroll in an office with leather furnishings and accolades on the wall? Is it that others seek you out to speak with you and fawn over you when you are in attendance? Is it having a full calendar? Is it a special trip overseas as a *thank you for your service*? Is it a PhD or other higher levels of learning after your name? Is success being on the radio, and TV, or having a high number of followers on Twitter? Is it being asked to open or close a gathering in prayer or give a word?

Oh be careful!

Defined, measurable points are good to gauge growth and further the vision toward accomplishment. Detailing achievable goals are good for forward motion. However,

God has a different definition of success. It is obedience.

You received a call on your life to establish a nonprofit. You take steps to enjoin others in the cause. You sought funding. And then nothing happens. The dream dies.

Or the ministry is established only to flounder and close due to myriad of reasons. The vision fails.

As a leader you will question if you discerned correctly. You will seek answers. "Should I have…?" "What if I…?" "If only…" "They should have…" A better way of thinking is this: "God, I was obedient to what you asked of me. I will celebrate that You called me, You directed me. It is not up to me to determine what is success and what is not." What? You read it right. It is *not* up to you to define what is successful. God asks for obedience. We have no idea why God does what He does or does not do.

Is God your God or not? Read about Shadrach, Meshach, and Abednego (Daniel 3:16-18). If God allows you to be burned in the fiery furnace and you can still say He is your God, THAT is obedience. Being truly bent to the will of God is real success. It does not make sense to our minds when ministry stops. It looks, feels, and sounds like a massive loss. Be comforted, still good and faithful servant, in a job well done for the season it was to be.

PONDER: Am I ready if and when it comes time to stop the ministry?

How will I view this occurrence?

Am I more content with success or with obedience to God?

Other ideas:

Now APPLY.

119. *Takers*

These types of people are very friendly. They have strengths. They could be a great asset to the ministry. You are willing to pour time and training into this person. But nothing comes of your investment in them. They are takers: taking whatever is of benefit to them and giving nothing in return.

Be watchful. They come with many bells and whistles, and on paper looks magnificent. But they have bounced from ministry to ministry, taking advantage of what is offered and using it to leverage their position in the community or for their own agenda.

They have no intention of committing to the mission of your organization.

Expect them to step up to show their intentions working in some capacity for some time before you let them into your vault of valued knowledge. They may use it against you or commandeer it as if it was their own.

PONDER: Have we let a taker into our confidence?

What damage did you do or are they doing?

What is the plan to prevent others like them from invading?

Other thoughts:

Now APPLY.

120. *Thesaurus And Editing*

As a leader you must write many types of documents; letters of solicitation, thank you letters, reports, newsletters, appeals, grant applications, procedures, processes, narratives, stories, testimonies and more. Get familiar with the thesaurus. Read other's writings to see what works. There is a myriad of templates on line and examples to review and utilize.

Once you have written a piece, have a team of one or two who are good at reviewing, proofread the document for the job. There are those in your ministry who are good at this and would enjoy volunteering. Be sure you are allowing time for the editing. I was putting together information for small businesses that would be sponsors of our advance training meetings. I had a potential sponsor I wanted to share the concept with. I drafted a solicitation letter and asked a talented volunteer to read it. They said that what I had written was not conveying what I said was the point. They offered to edit. I knew this was good. They took it home, took a full weekend to rewrite the letter, and provided a much better rendition of what I had created.

Many times what is in my head and what I write are not the same. To the reader as well as the consumer who will receive my missive, it must be clear, simple, and supported. Remember, no one has a long attention span anymore. Two or three paragraphs, is already too long for many.

When I have jumped ahead and posted without editing, there have been missteps, errors in spelling and more. This is not a professional way to present the ministry or yourself.

PONDER: What editing process do I have in our communications?

Have I ever had a team member show me spelling errors?

Am I good at writing communications or should this be shared with a more talented team member?

Do I humbly receive editing help?

Other thoughts:

Now APPLY.

121. *This Job Is Not All There Is: Heaven*

You are amazing! You have given your time, your talents, your energy: sweat equity, as I call it. Bravo! The world is changed because of you. Do not ever doubt lives have been impacted by you pressing forward. All ministries end, whether in a year or one hundred years. Do not compare your accomplishments with others. You have done well, good and faithful servant.

Remember there will always be more to do. There will always be the poor and needy. Remember you and I are a mess in our rebellious, sinful state and Jesus came to rescue you and me to take us to be with Him in heaven for eternity. I must be heavenly minded. As a leader in a Christian non-profit I know the end of my story and I will be with God. So on the job be sure to encourage your team to count the blessings of God, to yearn for the future when there will be no more hunger, nor thirst, and to remember that God will wipe away every tear (Revelation 7:16-17).

We will rejoice with the great multitude that no one can count, from every nation, tribe, people and language before the throne of and in front of Jesus saying 'Amen! Praise and glory and wisdom and thanks and honor and power and strength be to our God for ever and ever. Amen' (Revelation 7:9-12).

PONDER: Do I know how to be heavenly minded?

What do I need to study for that focus?

Am I fulfilled in my work? Do I know, really know, God is pleased with me?

Other thoughts:

Now APPLY.

122. Threats: External, Outside the Organization

The times, they are changing. Over the years the ministry has been operating, the level of pain the clients bring has increased. The levels of knowledge the volunteers bring have changed. It is vital that, as the leader, the top dog, you are aware of the cultural changes and not be buried so deeply in the daily work that you can't *see* what's out there.

In addition, the political climate is volatile. There are no guarantees that the government will always support christian organizations including churches. Laws and court rulings may hamper the ministry's effectiveness. Do not place your security in anything other than God. Be aware of what respected, national Christian leaders are saying. Be aware of what your community climate is. If possible,

be a part of the dialogue so others learn about christian organizations and the valid impact yours has.

Attend networking meetings. Be present. Build relationships. Be a witness representing your clients, your investors, your mission.

As the leader, you may not have regular contact with those who receive the care of your agency. Get outside your office, mingle, listen. Ask your staff to give you testimonies of what is coming through the doors.

PONDER: Do we survey our clients, team and community about the programs?

Does the Board address issues that are political, financial, and cultural issues that may impact the ministry?

Have I made the Board aware of changes that may impact our work?

Other ideas:

Now APPLY.

123. Threats: Inside the Ministry

Disruptions in relationships happen. Christian work is not immune from this. Every day the staff and volunteers are challenged in their personal lives which can affect their work. Additionally, the work they do is stressful.

Take time to pour into your staff and volunteers. Make sure they are having enough time away to recharge. Have an open-door policy. While, it is wonderful if they pour into you, it is not your role to be needy. If they assume you are struggling, they are more apt to withhold important information that is critical for the health of the business. Vulnerable—yes. Authentic—yes. Portray being in charge and capable of the challenge the work has for you and your team. These are WORK relationships. Work is the common factor.

Some folks come with a style of working that is contrary to yours and to others. Communication is so important. Empower your workers with the right to establish boundaries with each other, not just with the clients. Do not unintentionally put expectations on them that are not in the job description. For instance: birthday gifts. Some may have the love language of giving. Others do not. Is this an expectation that one must spend money on others? What about your organization's fundraisers? Are the staff to attend all or none? Who pays for their tickets? People's desk contents: is it for an individual's use or to be shared? Put it back where it was.

And the dreaded office microwave and refrigerator. What are rules for use and cleaning? If a worker does not attend to her week of cleaning, is this a cause for concern? If so, it needs to be added to the job description as well as the staff handbook. Strife can be avoided if rules are identified, communication is open, and review of rules are regular. All may not like each rule, but organizationally, things flow more smoothly.

Ask for input on what future changes need to be made.

PONDER: How are conflicts between coworkers handled?

Is this written down?

What are the values and what is the culture of the work community at your nonprofit?

Other thoughts that kicked up considering this topic:

Now APPLY.

124. Threats: Internal And Dangerous

Our organization has strong language in its job descriptions and in its overview, application and contract for volunteers. The language unequivocally states the necessity of an active relationship with Jesus Christ as Lord and Savior before consideration for employment or volunteering. It is not a prerequisite for our clients. We seek to be clear about who we are and who we care for in the ministry's programs. This has provided clear documentation when interviewing interested parties. Those who volunteer are in agreement with what we are and what we do. Prevention is vastly better than being infected by someone who we allowed in our midst and harming them when it is necessary to terminate their involvement.

When the ministry is asked to speak, we discuss with the caller what the goal is for the engagement and who the audience will be. Sharing our faith in God, the representative then has the opportunity to determine if our organization is the best fit. We have been turned away, but that is a good thing. If our beliefs or style is not a match, then we certainly do not want to be a stumbling point.

Repeatedly we hear how safe the clients, staff, and volunteers feel because they know the expectations and limits of individual roles in the ministry. Interested parties have appreciated our transparency and turned aside to serve in other ways, grateful for the interaction with us.

It does more harm to all if we are not obvious in our mission, vision and values.

PONDER: When have we let someone into our midst who did not truly understand who we are and what we do?

Was there harm to them and/or the ministry?

What steps are in place to provide clear information about the organization?

Am I as a leader, confident in myself to have difficult discussions with interested parties who may or may not fit our culture?

Other Thoughts:

Now APPLY.

125. Volunteers: It Costs Them Time And Money To Serve

Dependable. Always there. I can count on… These persons are the backbone of our organization. Quiet operators. Loyal. Dedicated. Invaluable. If you have a precious piece of jewelry, would you leave it out in the rain? Protect your assets—your people. These hard workers don't want public fanfare; in fact, many would be embarrassed by it. But one-to-one, showing appreciation, taking time to sit with them and hear their thoughts, showing you know and care and value them is important because *they are important.*

They work for the cause and love you as their leader.

They are often part of the organization for years. The success of the ministry is their success. But don't take them for granted. Ever.

Capture the hours given by volunteers. Our volunteers are an army of wisdom, empowerment, patience, and grace. And all of us must walk this earth earning and paying our way. They give up their time to serve at the Eve Center. Many give hours and hours. Over 10,000 hours of service last year were given. Multiply that by the minimum wage of your state, all given with joy to serve God in ministry. And that doesn't truly capture the value of this incredible gift of time. We could never replace any of these with staff. Men, too, serve in program support, on the Board, in fundraising, technical support, design and graphics, and photography. Then add the cost of gas, etc., to get to and from the Eve Center, time in prayer for the ministry and the clients; time is also given to prepare and to deepen their knowledge of issues that have come with the clients. It is a huge donation our volunteers make. Yet everyone comes because the ministry work fills their soul need to serve others in this life community.

Develop a time sheet for each volunteer. Put in categories of assistance such as:

1. Taking training
2. Client care
3. Office support
4. Research
5. Prayer

6. Representing ministry at meeting
7. Other lines for things they may do outside the office for the ministry

Recommend the forms be turned into the staff in a timely fashion. Total the hours and honor the volunteer. These hours show investment of time. Donors are delighted to see the full picture of all that goes on at your organization.

PONDER: Do we capture the hours given by volunteers?

Do I report this internally and to the community? (This is a great way to thank your volunteers).

What can I as the leader do to appreciate my laborers in the ministry?

Other thoughts:

Now APPLY.

126. Watch Woman On The Tower

Besides being a vision keeper, I am the vision protector. It is my responsibility to stand the line on the watchtower and be in communication with God. He is EL ROI —the God who sees. I join Him to glean what He foresees so that I am able to lead well. In this way, I perceive potential disruptors and communicate this to the Board and staff. For example, there may be one who wants into ministry, wants in through our walls, who intends to steal our materials. They want to know what we do and how we do it and *"Why can't you just show me, give me a copy to read?"* This stealth invader has their own agenda and will abuse us for their own purposes. Or there is the person who agrees with Biblical peer counseling but do they *"really believe in the inerrant word of God?"* This person could cause disunity over foundational principles through false belief. Or the sweet one who tugs at our hearts. They love Jesus and wants to give back. Can they be trained as a peer counselor?

In our interview process we ask if there is anything, any crisis, and behavior that will prohibit them from modeling healthy, adult Christianity at this time. It is not in their past—we accept that for we all have our story of redemption. This is the right here, right now. If they share they are in the midst of a crisis or consuming conflict. It is our right, our place, to determine if an applicant will be more of a client than a volunteer before each candidate is accepted. That is why we have face-to-face interviews of every applicant and also call references. We want to insure we do no harm to the applicant by placing unattainable expectations on them, burdening the staff with a volunteer who clearly needs support as a client first, or pair them with clients for whom they cannot be a dependable presence.

So be watchful, listening to the ground for steps toward your tower. Not all are friendly.

PONDER: Am I easily run over by 'stealth invaders'?

Have I or my team allowed a client or others to absorb our time, drawing from our well of skills only to take them and run?

Other thoughts that kicked up considering this topic:

Now APPLY.

127. *Watch The Um, And Like*

Add to this list *you know*. We hear these additives all the time from TV, radio, friends, family, and work. The lesson is:

tighten up your speech.

FROM CLOUDS TO CONCRETE

It is not professional to have these useless words coming out of your mouth. Take a pause to order your words. Nerves are usually the cause of mangled speech. That and we repeat what we hear, you know? Um, like I was saying... dude...

Listen to others. Then listen to yourself. If need be, adopt a consequence for every time you utter one:

1. Have someone verbally hit the buzzer by saying *erhh* like a buzzer when you use a filler word or sound. You will get so annoyed you will stop.
2. Money—make it cost you a dollar for every unprofessional word. That may sound high but the change won't come without pain.
3. Prepare before replying. Instead of saying, ummm, say "I'm thinking." Sometimes there is pressure to respond. You need to, and have the right to, pause to think about an answer.
4. Let someone else answer so you can decide if you really need to reply at all. Be more grown-up than the grown-ups. Eliminate the junk in your language.

PONDER: Is my public speaking slang or proper English?

Have I listened to myself?

What steps do I need to add to rectify this, 'um, like' thing?

Other thoughts:

Now APPLY.

128. What's my point? Personal or organizational? Or God?

As founder, or leader, of a Christian nonprofit, why are you doing what you do? Are you personally doing it to make up to God for some past sin? Are you trying to earn favor with family or friends so they respect you and look up to you? Are you staying busy in God work so as not to face close relationships like your marriage, parents, siblings, or friends who know you well?

Are you sincerely working hard to further the vision for the ministry, without a back-story agenda? Remember rare is the leader who has a simple call from God. The world and the Christian world is suspicious of authenticity and simplicity. Folks dig for the real story, the real dirt. Can you be trusted? Have you done something horrible in the past that explains it? The world just doesn't trust it especially if it is of God. You need to *check yourself* as well. If, like my story for years (see history) prior to surrendering to Christ, you are in the cause for self-assurance, self-fulfillment then your work won't last. *You* won't last for the long haul. This is because you will fail yourself just as I did. I could not keep up with the load of responsibility I placed on myself. There are many Christians who provide wonderful works for social justice agendas. Many 'do for God', not as He has directed. The degrees of difference between Christ-focused and fix-it-focused work multiply in time. The best way is to point to God: Serving God by working in the organization, I grow in relationship to Him and His people.

PONDER: Why doesn't the world accept God's call on my life?

Have I unloaded all the worldly reasons I may be in ministry?

Have I allowed God's refinement of me?

Other ideas:

Now APPLY.

129. What's The Point? Lessons To Be Learned

There are times when I have wondered, what's the point? Clients contact us for help. Some don't return calls or show up for appointments. Some don't listen to the free, caring, wise counsel they receive. Some just want to complain and grouse. Some want to blame everyone else without taking any responsibility for either what happened or what needs to change. Some just suck the life out of their peer counselors. Some challenge our procedures and want the rules bent just for them. Some have had so much assistance that they can repeat back what doctors, friends, pastors, and therapists have told them, yet they don't do any of it. The walking wounded are everywhere, and face it, the world isn't getting any nicer. So what's the point? Answer: Look up. Yes, look up to the Lord. Read about Elijah (1 Kings 19:10), who felt all alone and beaten down as if all was for naught.

Data analysis is very important. Purposefully capture what is happening in your ministry. How do you capture qualitative change like emotions, coping skills, relationships with God? Develop a grid about where a client begins in order to capture qualitative changes through their time in counsel, their emotions, coping skills and relationship to God are just a few things likely to change. Have them choose the degree is in trouble on a scale of 1-10. After receiving services, ask them if their life has improved on the same scale of 1-10. This puts quantitative data together for you to see how change is happening. Ask the client each time to give you a statement about how they are feeling/coping. You will hear pain at first and maybe hear hope now that they are in your care. After care you will hear that, yes, things are looking up. Ask for suggestions about any improvements to the ministry that can be made for future ministry clients. This gives you points to evaluate progress and growth.

You can gather points of evaluation. You can remember what the point is, the vision God gave you.

PONDER: How does my ministry capture improvements in the lives of clients?

Who is responsible for the statistics such as age and education of the clients for the ministry?

What insight does the team receive from client input?

Now APPLY.

130. *When It Is Time To Go*

Ministries are often born of a vision to change the world for the better in one form or another. Due to the tax laws of the United States, in order to deduct donations, the ministry must become a tax-exempt entity. In order for that to be approved by the Internal Revenue Service, a minimum of three board members must be appointed, bylaws adopted, and filings and fees are paid to the government. While the visionary is usually the Founder and the Director, they are *hired* by and answerable to the Board. Even a leader who receives no remuneration is still working for the Board. The Board is required to ensure the nonprofit is fulfilling its mission, raising funds to ensure sustainability, and not doing anything illegal. Simple enough. But with each human comes a different opinion about how these roles are to be walked out.

The Board and the Director should work together and be unified in the steps to be taken. *Should* is the operative word.

It is imperative that the Board members support, love on, and be there for the Director.

Unfortunately, many Board members are absent, only giving their name and no time to the board responsibilities. This leaves the director feeling unsafe, unsupported, and at times misunderstood. I have watched as several Christian ministries have been torn apart, sending the Director away even though they were the founder, due to conflicts. A Board and a Director should model a healthy, engaged, communicative relationship. They need each other to survive and grow.

When this godly design is swinging wildly out of control, damage is bound to result. If you are a Director, who may be facing departure under duress, seek the truth: Is it a power play? Is it personal? Is it simply time to pass the baton of leadership, and you haven't faced the fact the ministry has outgrown you? Do not prolong the agony. Be proactive in taking the high road. Bow out, leaving the ministry intact. If the whole point of doing anything and everything to date was for the mission, then remember that is the point of it all. You may have to be sacrificial and step away.

Write up your *press release*. This is what you will tell everyone over and over again as to why you are leaving. There will be those who dig for the dirt of what happened. Be a leader, model the best interests of those who receive the care. Then go grieve in a safe, confidential place. My heart aches for you.

PONDER: Have you ever been pointed to as the one *responsible* for causing a difficult situation in ministry?

What was going on and how did you handle it?

Is there any undercurrent of dissension in the ministry on any level?

How is my relationship with the Board? Healthy and balanced or not?

How do you discern when to defend or when to surrender?

Other thoughts:

Now APPLY.

131. *Who Do You Think You Are?*

Insecurity is a real struggle. The devil has an ongoing whisper in my ear "Who do you think you are? You know nothing!" This incessant chirping hovers just off my right shoulder at times. Then I follow it up: "I should have done…" "I didn't know to…" "It won't be as good as if I had…" "No one told me…" NO! Stop that! I must change the unsolicited tape that plays in my mind. It is vital to focus on Philippians 4: 6-8:

> *Do not be anxious about anything, but in everything, by prayer and petition, with thanksgiving, present your requests to God. And the peace of God which transcends all understanding, will guard your hearts and your minds in Christ Jesus. Finally, brothers (and sisters) whatever is true, whatever is noble, whatever is right, whatever is pure, whatever is lovely, whatever is admirable – if anything is excellent or praiseworthy – think about such things,*

I am a beloved daughter of the Risen Lord, chosen by Him before the world was made. I am holy in His eyes without fault. I stand before God covered in His love because of what Christ did. And NOTHING and NO ONE can change that. I was called by God, and given the vision for the ministry. I am human—God is I AM (Exodus 3:14). He equips me, He orders my steps. He is the ONLY ONE to whom I give account. I know who I am and whose I am. Do you?

PONDER: What thoughts challenge my safety and security?

What is my identity?

Can I stop the downward spiral of attacking thoughts?

How do I do that?

When am I most susceptible to bad thinking?

Other thoughts:

Now APPLY.

132. Who Is Responsible?

When something happens, a death, a wreck, a divorce, everyone wants to know whose fault it is. "You must have done something wrong." "You should have…" Loads of guilt is cast about like a feather pillow piling downy shame anywhere it might fall. This happens whenever change occurs. Our ministry has had to make some tough but God-led decisions about how it was to grow in a managed fashion.

This meant letting go of a partnership that was successful catering to many clients in a godly way. Yet, that season was over, and a meeting was set to share how wonderful it had been and how God was calling our organization in a different direction going forward. Shortly after the meeting to announce the changes, a communication string began—digging for cause, searching for who did what. It was as if the former partner just couldn't believe that what we said was the simple truth—God was calling us to refine what we were doing in order to grow further as He directed.

Rather than get into a defensive mode and debate it with different others,

we simply repeated what we had put in writing and left it there.

Take the high road, friends. Do not get into making up what isn't there. Do not find fault. Do not repeat what is not affirming, uplifting, or of God. It only prolongs the processes and sows seeds of discord to soothe someone else's nerves.

PONDER: Has our organization received an unforeseen communication about change?

How did we handle it?

Has our nonprofit had to make decisions based on what God was directing that affected others?

How did we communicate it to those affected, our team, the community?

Other thoughts:

Now APPLY.

133. ZZZZ....

And so I close.

Some time ago, I was in the elevator at Cincinnati Children's Medical Center going to visit a volunteer whose child was receiving care. What does one say to a coworker, friend, a mother, whose little one is ill and afraid?

What do any of us say to those who are struggling? Yet our sweet, loving, nurturing *Abba* God knew ahead of time I would be there in that elevator between floors wondering how to be there for her.

There was a glass covering over a bulletin board on the elevator. Inside were notices about various clinics, nutrition guides, etc. Right to the side in simple black print on a piece of white paper was written the following:

Have courage for the great sorrows of life and patience for the small ones.

And when you have laboriously accomplished your daily task,

Go to sleep in peace.

God is awake.

Victor Hugo

Ministry work is hard. Christian nonprofit leadership is hard. Yet it is also soul filling. It is intense and pleasurable. It is being closer to God by being in His will, working the plan together. My prayer for you is that you ponder with God all He would have you learn. Dream as you look toward the clouds of heaven. Then walk it out here on earth on your concrete road of life - Wildly with abandon, APPLY!

About the Author

CINNY ROY is the Founder and Executive Director of the Eve Center, which promotes healing and growth for women through biblical, no cost, safe and confidential peer counseling and training. She attended Cincinnati Christian University and is an Ohio licensed professional clinical counselor, as well as trainer, writer, and consultant.

Index

Numbers are Leadership Life Lesson numbers, not page numbers.

Leadership:
4, 6, 8, 17, 22, 24, 25, 26, 27, 38, 42, 44, 47, 48, 49, 58, 59, 61, 62, 66, 68, 69, 70, 74, 77, 84, 86, 88, 89, 93, 94, 98, 99, 106, 109, 113, 115, 118, 126, 127, 130, 132, 133

Personal:
2, 7, 12, 16, 20, 23, 39, 45, 51, 55, 56, 59, 63, 73, 78, 84, 87, 93, 103, 112, 133

Procedures & Protocol:
3, 11, 21, 28, 29, 31, 32, 34, 36, 40, 41, 52, 67, 80, 81, 84, 91, 95, 98, 107, 108, 110, 116, 120, 123, 129, 132

Relationship With:

    Board: 19, 53, 54, 64, 65, 73, 76, 86, 92, 96, 97, 104, 110, 113, 122, 130

    Clients & Community: 8, 5, 33, 36, 37, 39, 47, 52, 57, 60, 82, 83, 91, 102, 105, 111, 119, 124

    Volunteers & Staff: 1, 5, 9, 10, 13, 14, 19, 24, 25, 35, 36, 37, 46, 48, 49, 50, 55, 60, 71, 72, 79, 83, 84, 86, 90, 94, 98, 100, 101, 105, 106, 108, 119, 122, 123, 125, 129, 133

    God: 18, 30, 62, 63, 65, 84, 114, 116, 117, 118, 121, 128, 131, 133

www.ingramcontent.com/pod-product-compliance
Lightning Source LLC
Chambersburg PA
CBHW032115090426
42743CB00007B/360